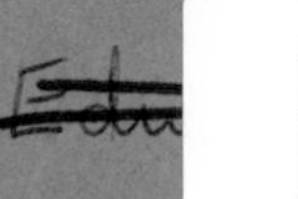

C000184349

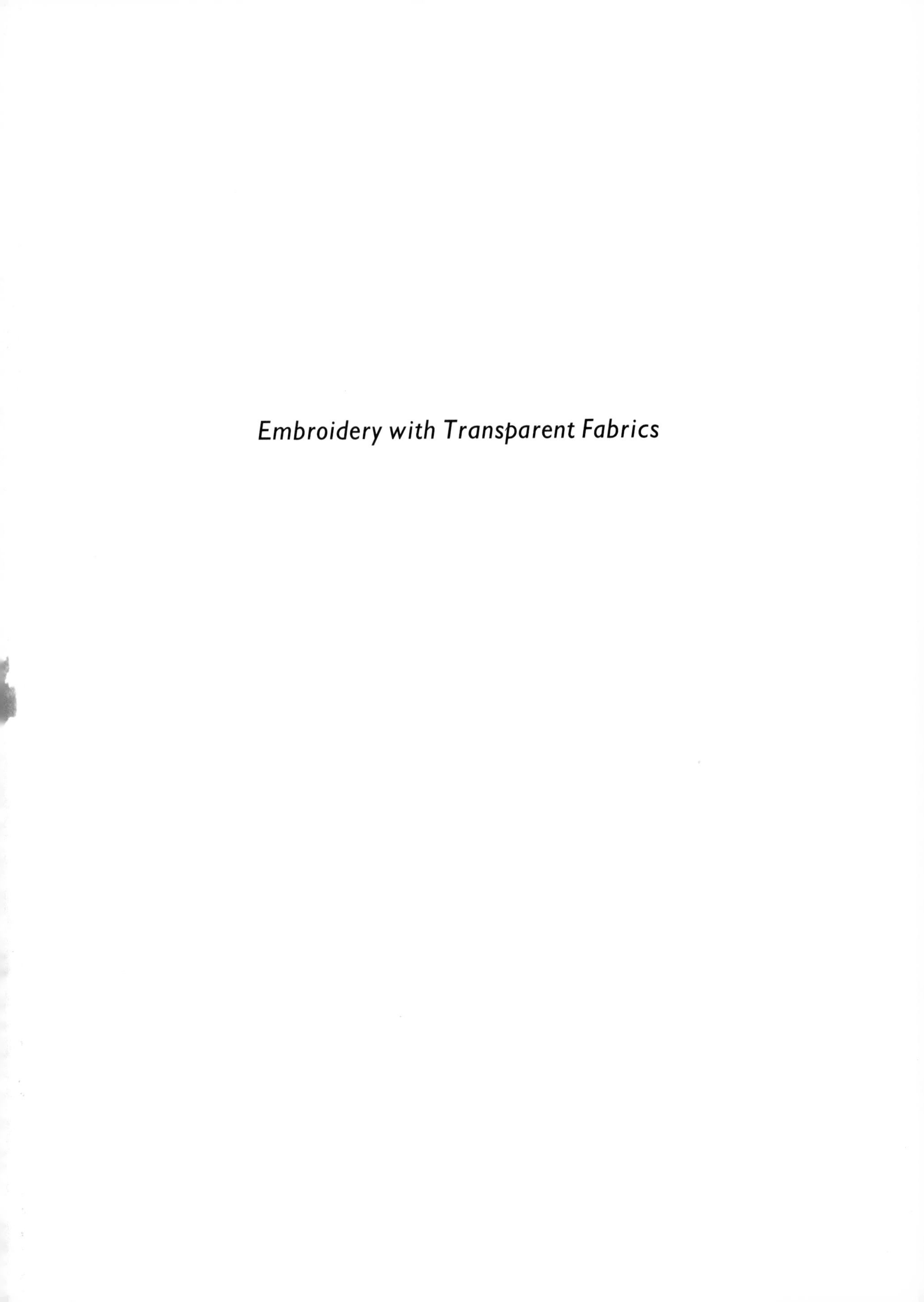

Embroidery with Transparent Fabrics

Sylvia Bramley

Embroidery with Transparent Fabrics

B. T. Batsford Ltd, London

Acknowledgment

I would like to express my thanks to all those people who have allowed their work to be photographed for the book. My thanks also to the many students at Bristol for their friendship and support. Finally my thanks to my husband for his help when things became tense.

Except where stated, all the embroideries, drawings and photographs are the work of the author.

Dedication
To Sam

First published 1989

ISBN 0 7134 5686 8

Typeset by Keyspools Ltd, Golborne, Lancs.
and printed in Great Britain by
Bath Press, Bath
for the publishers
B. T. Batsford Ltd
4 Fitzhardinge Street
London W1H 0AH

CONTENTS

INTRODUCTION

Although the title of this book uses the term 'transparent fabrics', most of the time it would be more correct to describe them as semi-transparent, or simply fine or sheer. All the fabrics, however, have a see-through quality which is exploited in both hand and machine embroidery techniques.

In order to make the book self-contained, there are chapters on design and techniques which could relate to embroidery in general, but here certain ideas are developed specifically in relation to transparent fabrics.

Fabrics such as cotton organdie, once used extensively for shadow work, tableware and for children's clothes, are nowadays not quite so easily obtainable. Silk organza, however, is still available and has the same fine weave, although its surface has a sheen compared with the matt finish of organdie. Many of today's fine fabrics are either completely synthetic, being made of nylon or polyester, or mixtures of synthetics and cotton silk or rayon. These mixtures combine delicacy with toughness, providing enormous possibilities for practical use as well as decorative finishes.

Many of the silk and nylon organzas have a crystal finish, or are woven to give 'shot' effects. They are dyed the most fabulous colours, from pale pastels to rich bronze-reds and vibrant turquoise.

Another fabric which comes into the category of 'transparent' is net, whether it is fine silk net or plastic garden net.

The pleasure of using these fine fabrics is most apparent when we are trying to create an atmosphere, or to show one colour lying behind another. Layers of materials can be used without the final effect being heavy or cumbersome. The fabrics can be folded, pleated or gathered, making textures and creating shadows to enrich a surface. Edges may be torn or frayed, or, in the case of synthetics, distorted with a hot iron or by being held near a candle flame. Some fabrics can be cut into strips, threaded in a needle and used as thread.

Working with these fine fabrics needs careful thought, particularly the purpose for which they are chosen. Edges

Machine embroidery and soluble fabric used to interpret olive trees

are sometimes difficult to handle, and, if turned under, the double layer will show. In purely creative work, such as panels, it may not be necessary to neaten edges, and frayed edges can have a charm of their own to be exploited.

This is an exciting area of embroidery, with endless scope for experiment. The ideas shown here are only a starting point, intended to stimulate and inspire the reader's own embroideries.

CHAPTER 1

Ideas and design

Fundamental to all arts and crafts should be a solid basis of good design. Contrary to what many people believe, design does not appear out of thin air but is the product of observation, awareness, deliberate thought and, if we are lucky, the occasional flash of inspiration.

Observing and recording ideas

A mind-shattering idea may be something we all hope for, but waiting around for it to happen is non-productive. Even if it did happen, it would require a lot of research and development before becoming a fact. In the meantime, ideas for designs can, with a little imagination and thought, be found all around us. This is not to say that solutions are ready-made and waiting to be used, but by training ourselves to really look we can become more aware of the elements which contribute to a design. We can learn to appreciate how important quite small differences are to a satisfactory arrangement.

We are bombarded every day by visual images: natural ones which change with the weather and the seasons, and man-made ones such as the towns we live in or travel through, the goods we buy to use in our homes, and particularly advertising images. None of the man-made items just 'happen', and innumerable changes are made before the final decisions are taken. Looking at a well-thought-out piece of work, whether it be a painting, a dress or a piece of embroidery, it is easy to forget that decisions

1 *Images surround us. The silhouettes of trees in winter show a rich source for a variety of lines*

2 *These cascading leaves could be a starting point for an embroidery to be worked on two layers of transparent fabrics*

had to be made and problems solved before a final conclusion was reached.

Sometimes at an exhibition one hears the remark, 'I could do that!' This might be true, for copying is easy when the main trials and errors have already been worked through, but most craftspeople realize that there is much more to be gained by combining original ideas with good technique.

Sketchbooks

A sketchbook is an invaluable piece of equipment for an embroiderer – a place to record ideas and drawings, as distinct from designing, which is a conscious and deliberate use of those ideas. This does not mean that one must be a superb draughtsman or painter; the sketchbook may be used for jotting down the briefest observations.

Drawing trains us to observe not only the obvious, what we think we know, but also the details: how shadows create form; how leaves join stems. The angle made by a leaf joining a twig is often the same as the angle made by the twig joining a branch. This kind of observation may not necessarily relate to a specific piece of work, but when it comes to making a design from leaves, these details are known and taken into account.

Drawing for drawing's sake, even if one is not very proud of the result, gradually builds up the power of observation. Not every drawing will be perfect or a success; indeed, it should not be so, for that would stop experimentation. A sketchbook is as personal as a diary; instead of recording events and impressions, it should be a record of ideas and developments. It is basic to the development from the first idea to starting to stitch.

Apart from drawings, other information can be stored within a sketchbook, such as unusual colour combinations found in backgrounds or odd corners of advertisements.

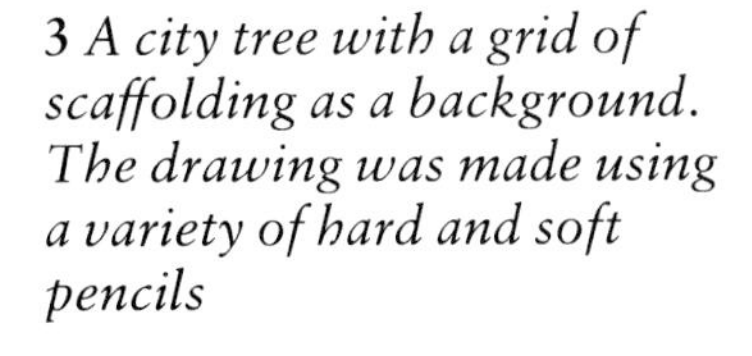

3 *A city tree with a grid of scaffolding as a background. The drawing was made using a variety of hard and soft pencils*

These colours can often be achieved by placing one transparent fabric on top of or behind another. Matching threads and fabrics to these unusual mixtures can sometimes be instrumental in starting off a new piece of work; at the very least, it makes you look at the subtleties of colour. I remember very clearly visiting an arboretum in the autumn and arriving home with my head full of the wonderful colours I had seen. I started to make a collection of threads of what I thought were the colours, but they did not seem quite right. So I looked at the collection of leaves I had gathered, and matched those with threads and fabrics; the difference was enormous, an exercise not to be forgotten. Mistakes like this are much easier to sort out on paper rather than when the work is in progress.

Pencils, felt tip pens and charcoal

Using pencils (from the H range for hard, stony effects, to the B range for blacker areas) can be a joy for one person but a positive nightmare for another. This a pity, for after all a drawing is only a piece of paper with marks on it.

Fortunately, pencils are not the only means of expressing ideas on paper. Felt tip pens are made in a variety of thicknesses and colours, and give a very direct mark which cannot be rubbed out but can be drawn over or cross-hatched, or drawn over a wash of watercolour. Charcoal is another medium, not suitable if fine detail is required but marvellous for strong, bold drawing.

Pastels

Soft pastels are an excellent medium for putting down blocks of colour; they are very direct and immediate in their impact. One colour can be smudged into another by rubbing with a finger, which gives impressions rather than detail. This method is particularly useful for subjects like gardens, where one plant lies behind another and edges are blurred. Pastels can be used for linear drawing, or, by holding the pastel on its side, stroked onto the paper in broad bands almost like paint.

It is important in this type of drawing to look for tones, the lightness or darkness of the subject, particularly the shadows. It is interesting to look at the paintings of Monet and to note how many rich, dark colours he uses in his shadows. Recently I wanted to darken an area of shadow but did not have the correct-coloured pastel, so I used a deep violet simply to darken the tone. The effect was vibrant, and suggested a way of using thread and stitch in a similar fashion.

Photographing in black and white, or photocopying pastel drawings, gives a surprising impression of stitching which might be used for furthering an idea. Many people use a camera to record impressions, and it is a useful way to capture a moment in time. Whichever medium is used (and, of course, not everyone has the same preference), thinking on paper will carry the original idea one stage on. The colours, textures, lines and shapes which appear on paper from inks, pencils, pastels, etc. may of themselves provide alternative ways of interpreting the original idea. One thing is certain, the final result will be personal and individual.

Designing

Over the past few years, embroiderers have become more aware of possible sources for design. No longer is it regarded as slightly peculiar to collect rusty tins for their colour, crumpled paper for its texture, or string for its linear qualities, but there does still seem to be some difficulty in knowing what to do with these ideas which initially excite us. How is the colour recorded? Does the paper stay just crumpled paper, or does it become shapes for abstract textures? And what can be done with lines, however interesting? Already, by asking ourselves these questions, important elements of design have been mentioned: (1) colour, (2) shape, (3) texture, (4) line. Let us add two more: (5) pattern and (6) proportion. Designing is about the conscious, deliberate use and manipulation of these elements.

Let us consider these sources for design in more detail:

A rusty tin

A rusty tin might have exciting colour, but, unless it is looked at carefully and its proportions noted, tiny accent colours could be overlooked and the whole thing simply dismissed as 'rust-coloured'. Careful, deliberate study might reveal colours such as burnt orange (30%), bright yellow (10%), yellow ochre (20%), turquoise (5%), violet (5%), bronze (10%), grey (20%).

This group of colours need no longer be related to a rusty tin, but could be used, in these proportions, for an abstract pattern or for a woodland in autumn. Further colour experiments could be carried out by mixing the colours with white to dilute them into pastels, or mixing them with black

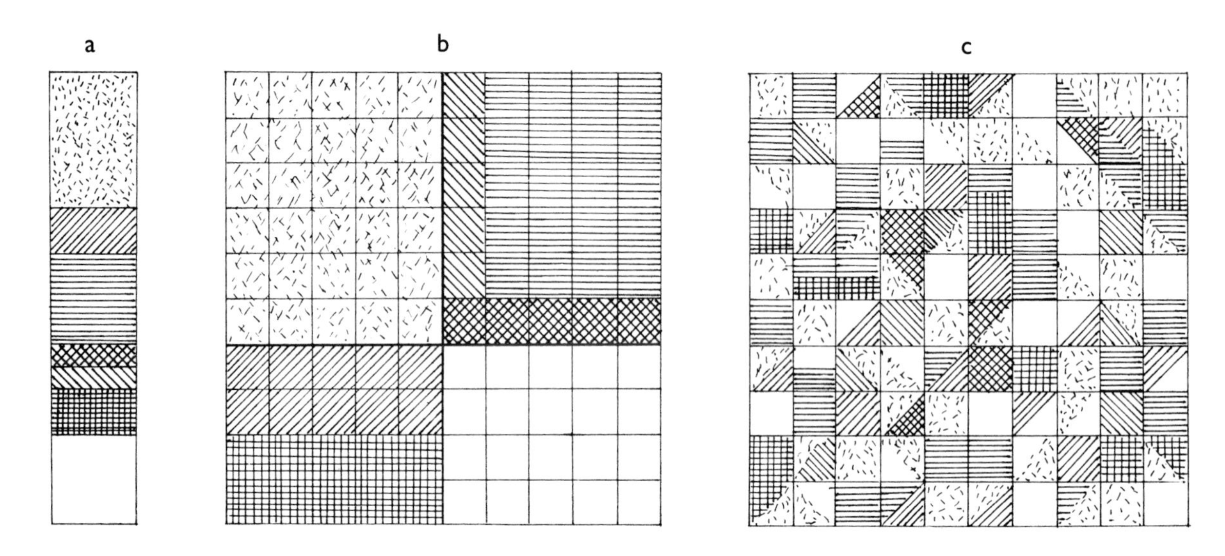

4 *Colours found on a rusty tin*
a *The chart shows the colour proportions:*

burnt orange	*30%*
bright yellow	*10%*
yellow ochre	*20%*
turquoise	*5%*
violet	*5%*
bronze	*10%*
grey	*20%*

b *The same percentage of colours divided over a grid of 100 squares*
c *The same proportion of colours but spread in a different way over 100 squares*

to turn them into shades. All manner of experiments with fabric and thread might follow.

A piece of crumpled paper

Looking at crumpled paper, first of all the crease lines could be drawn, taking care to observe the different widths. Then the shapes could be drawn, taking care to observe the very small shapes as well as the bigger ones. As with colour, observing small variations can make designs interesting instead of just bland. This does not mean that everything recorded has to be used for the purpose of the design. Some lines or shapes may be eliminated, but observations have been made and choices can follow.

With the lines and shapes drawn, decisions can be made whether the lines, or alternatively the shapes, might be textured. Here another element of design occurs, that of contrast. To have all the shapes and all the lines textured might be overdoing it, and leave nowhere for the eye to rest. This is not always the case; for instance, if the lines are textured but all of a neutral colour, they could contrast well with textured shapes in chosen colours. There are no absolutes in designing. Thankfully, there is room for all our varied preferences, but being aware of the elements of

5 a A line drawing of crumpled paper
b A group of shapes. These could be used for shadow quilting
c The lines have been emphasized
d A section has been chosen and the lines repeated, giving a feeling of rhythm

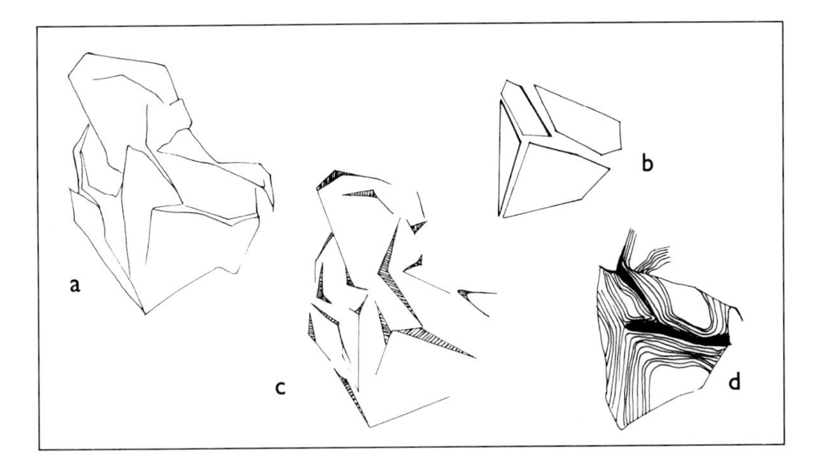

design and being willing to experiment and to take a second or third look can lead to much greater satisfaction.

A piece of string

If a piece of string is laid on paper, a line can be drawn along its contour and the paper can then be cut out along the line, giving two edges. This could be used as a template, drawing parallel lines first with equal distances, then with unequal spaces between. Repeating these lines with different thicknesses of pen nib, pencil, charcoal, pastel or with brush and paint will give a different appearance to the line and suggest different ways of interpreting it.

6 a A line taken from a piece of string is repeated regularly
b The lines are repeated with unequal distances between
c The line is moved sideways as well as up and down, creating irregular shapes

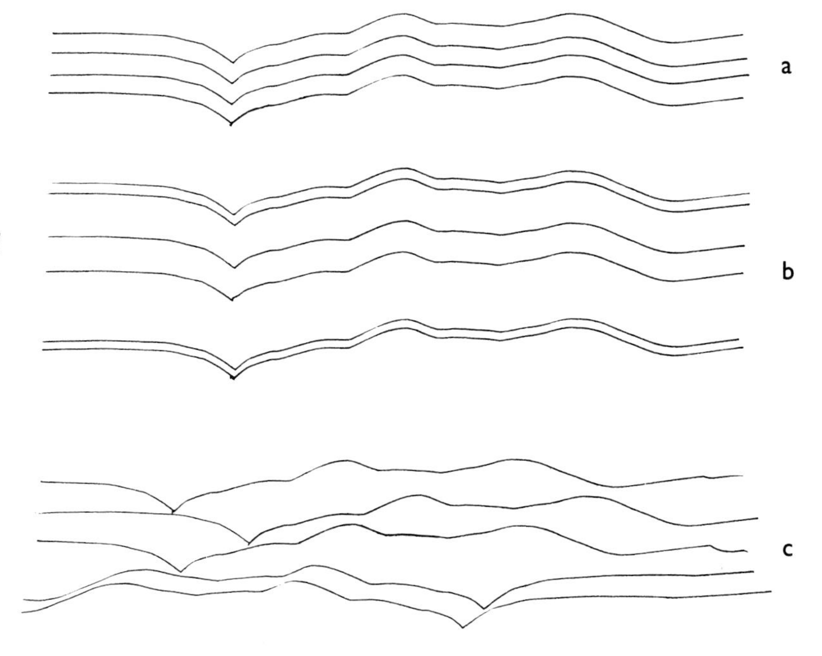

By moving the template up or down, interesting irregular lines can be drawn, the spaces between now becoming shapes.

From these three ordinary beginnings, it can be seen that a number of designs are ready to be pursued. The ideas which were the starting points, the rusty tin, the crumpled paper and the string, are no longer in evidence and it is time to consider the designs as one stage on towards starting a piece of embroidery.

Elements of design

As already stated, the elements of design consist of line, shape, colour, texture, pattern, proportion and contrast. These considerations, with their many combinations, are everywhere, but to recognize them, and to use them to transform the ordinary to the special, takes conscious thought. Particular care needs to be given to small changes, reducing a gap by a fraction, smoothing a curve, thinning or thickening a line. Saying that ideas for design are all around us is true, but even more so for those with the will to use those ideas.

Lines

Let us start with lines, and look at some everyday objects.

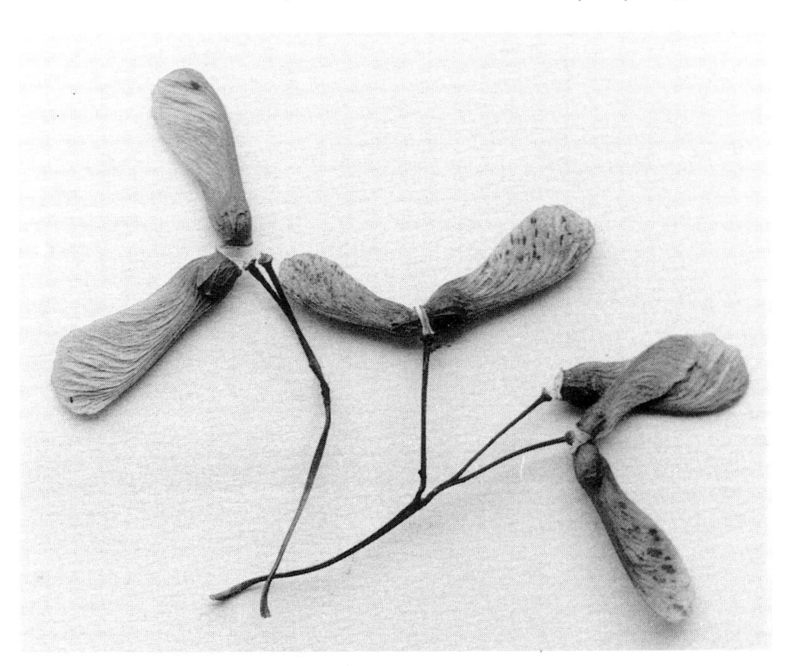

7 *Subtle series of lines can be found on sycamore seeds*

8 *This winter landscape is a mass of different lines, and at first sight could prove daunting*

9 *Abstracting some of the lines is a first move towards a working drawing*

Straight lines: Venetian blinds, fences, ploughing lines, lamp standards, particularly on motorways (these give a strong indication of perspective), railway lines, electricity pylons, trunks of trees, construction lines of buildings.

Curved lines: outlines of hills, rivers and streams, markings, such as on sycamore seeds and the edges of leaves.

Straight lines cross-hatched can give the impression of curves as well as create density. Horizontal and vertical lines can be crossed to make grids, on which so many patterns are based.

Now let us look at one group of lines and consider how they could be used as a source of design.

Venetian blinds

These are lines with a uniform thickness. They can be seen as uniform strips breaking up the view beyond. By providing neutral, quiet interludes, the view through them can be seen as broken areas of colour and texture. This could be a starting point for a design, for instance:

1 Areas of texture and flat areas could be noted.
2 Look for areas of light tone and areas of dark tone.
3 Does a prominent line appear and disappear?
4 As the outside is viewed through glass, is there any diffusion? (The different greens of a garden might merge together, while the colours of the flowers make areas of colour.)
5 Which area is the most important from a colour or textural point of view, and therefore likely to be the focal point?

10 *Different series of lines, some needing the precision of a ruler, others drawn freehand*

This is conscious thought and questioning about possibilities, but at this stage a few practical exercises are needed; it is impossible for most people to proceed beyond this stage by mental processes alone. This can also be a dangerous moment, as there is the urge to translate the excitement of the idea into fabric and thread. By all means, stitch a small sample – often in this moment of euphoria direct stitching may produce something fresh and uninhibited – but then it is advisable to stop and take stock, and to consider other possibilities. A few experiments allow ideas to develop and, just as important, mistakes to be made and reviewed. The development can sometimes be very surprising, leading to a satisfactory conclusion instead of jumping from the first idea to an obvious, and sometimes banal, end product. Equally, it must be stated, there is a danger of staying in the experimental stage too long and never resolving anything.

So what are the next stages? Here are a few suggestions. They are not the only ones and should be considered only as starting points:

1 Using a pencil or ballpoint pen, draw the lines for the Venetian blinds. In the spaces, block in the light, medium and dark areas. This can be done with solid areas or by cross-hatching.
2 Repeat exercise 1 but, instead of drawing the lines for the

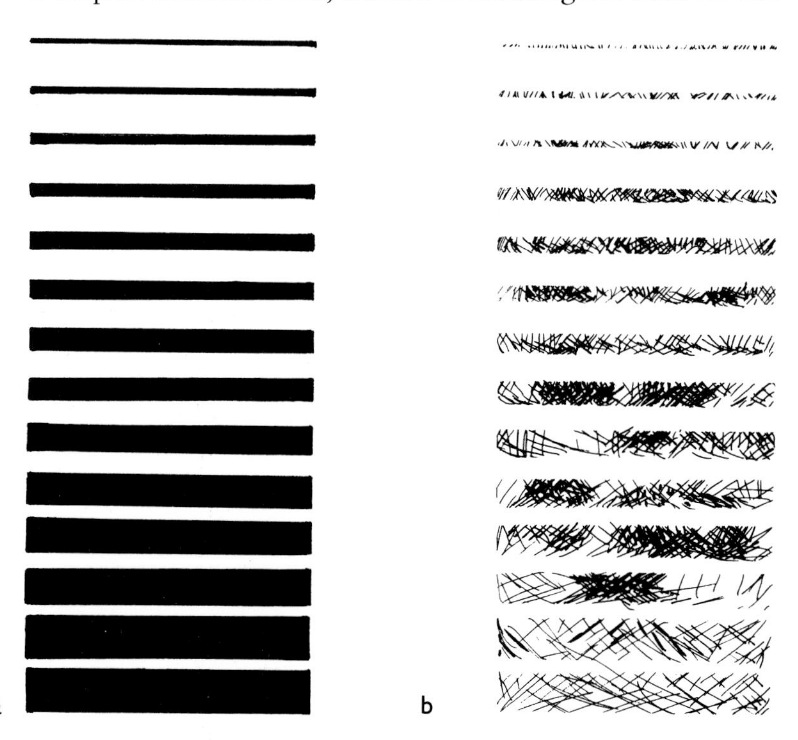

11 a *Using the Venetian blind idea to make a stencil. This makes a series of graduated stripes*
b *Stippling through the stencil gives the impression of looking through the blind to the view beyond*

blinds, simply leave the blinds as empty shapes, i.e. voiding the blind shape.

3 Using pastels, crayons, or sticking down bits of coloured paper, colour the view, referring to exercise 1 for the light and dark areas.
4 How are the blinds to be treated? These could be voided, or stitched, or applied as strips. Stick strips of paper down to see how they look, as they have a thickness of their own.

So far, the width of the blind slats and the width of the spaces between have been considered to be equal, but in fact they both vary according to how much the blind is open and where the viewer is standing. As we are now thinking in

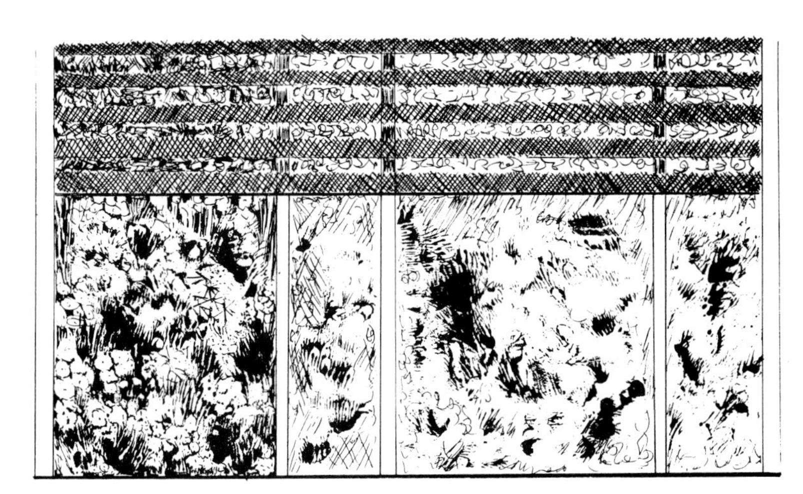

12 *A development of Fig. 11 through an open window*

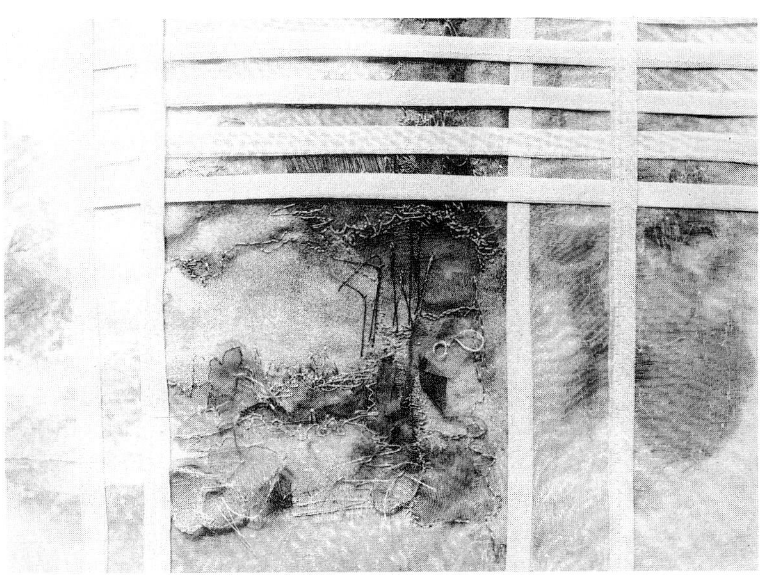

13 *A trial sample of how the idea might progress*

terms of a design, and not necessarily realism, this may not matter but it does provide another alternative.

The Venetian blind series of lines has been looked at head on as a two-dimensional pattern, but other series of lines show perspective indicating a third dimension, for example, ploughing lines in a field. If the field is undulating, the lines can form blocks of pattern, as can planted rows of vegetables or shrubs.

One memory I have is of rows of lavender in Provence, growing for the perfume trade, with a cornfield in front and dark green cypresses in the distance. The colours of golden yellow, lavender and dark green, and the striped pattern of receding lines created by the rows of lavender left a lasting impression. Although I have a photograph as a record, it is not the same as my own remembered image, which is more important for a creative piece of work than reproducing a photograph.

This is one more reason for making notes or drawings at the time; photographs are very useful, particularly for information, but the camera records everything within its range, and everything optically correct. It cannot record the emotions, or the selections and interpretations, that the eyes and brain together make. We probably all have the experience of photographing something like a ship at sea, knowing it to be huge, but the camera, being optically correct, shows the ship as a dot on the ocean. The eye sees the ship and the brain knows that it is large, and together our perception is that there is a large ship on the sea. By no means should the camera be under-valued; it can be of immense use as an aid to design, but it does not have to be copied slavishly.

Giving a line thickness can alter the quality completely. Think of a figure eight. This is very easy to draw in a single line where no thought is needed about one line crossing another. Thickening the line makes it much more important, and again the crossing seems to take care of itself.

When sets of parallel lines are drawn, more care needs to be taken where the lines cross. Decisions need to be made about which lines should be on top and which should be underneath. This is the basis of strapping and interweaving, and it is also a problem to be solved when working Italian quilting.

Whereas structural lines of buildings and Venetian blinds depend upon a really straight edge, freehand drawing adds another quality. Lines drawn and repeated, lines bending to

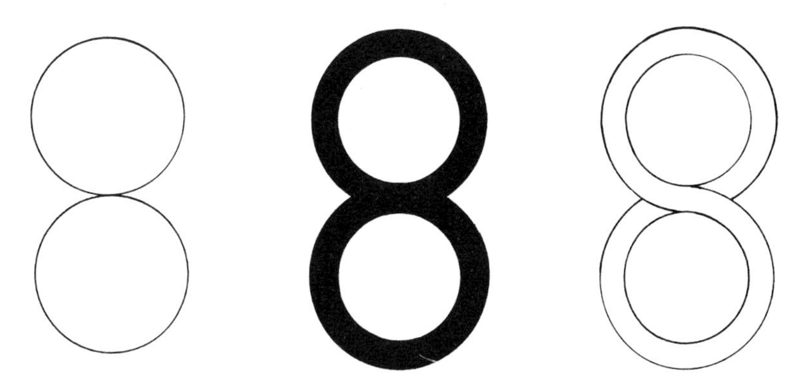

14 *When lines are drawn in parallel, care is needed where they cross*

make a zigzag, regular and irregular shapes with lines surrounding or swirling between, these are all useful doodles to increase one's awareness. Trying deliberately to draw a subtle line can be difficult, but the following ideas may be useful.

The first idea is similar to using the piece of string mentioned earlier. Use a piece of bark fallen from a tree (plane trees shed their bark) and draw along its edge onto a piece of thin card. Cut along the line, which will give two edges to use as a template. These lines can be repeated in parallel, with the same or differing spaces between, for one series, or the template can be moved along so that the lines are no longer parallel.

The second idea gives a similar result if no bark is available. Choose a letter and write it as irregularly as possible. Draw a line following the irregularities along the bottom of the letters. Cut along this line and use it in the same way.

These lines, as well as being used in parallel, can be crossed at different angles to make irregular grids.

15 *Making a subtle line by repeating a letter of the alphabet in an irregular way*

16 *The many shapes of pebbles on a beach*

Shapes

Natural forms

Shape is another important element of design. Many things are identified by shape and outline before examining the details. For instance, people have the same component parts but they all vary slightly, and it is this small variation of shape which enables us to recognize people we know from a distance.

We recognize leaves, shells, etc. under those headings but we also identify them and categorize them by their indiv-

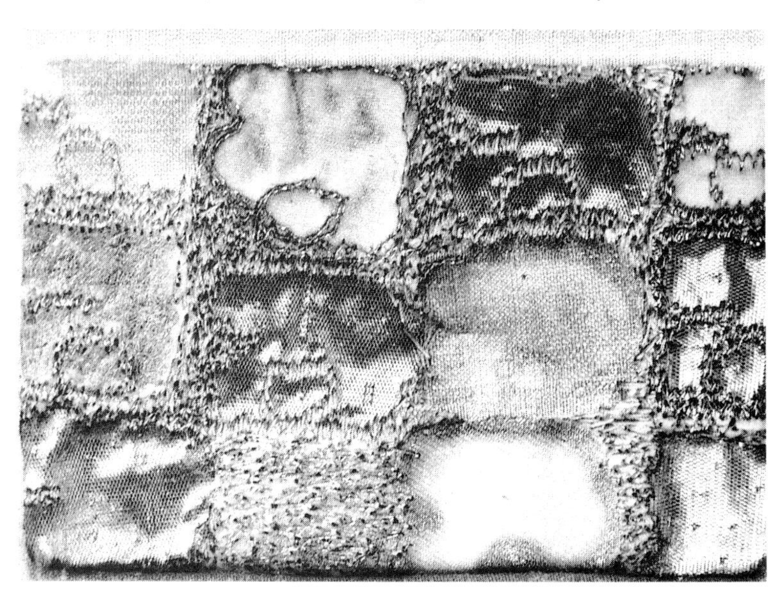

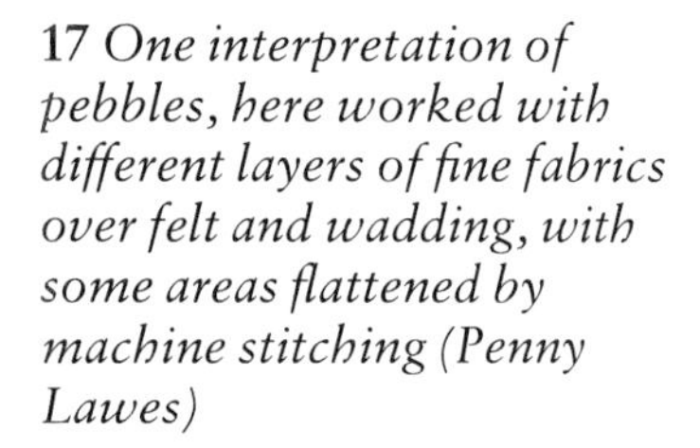

17 *One interpretation of pebbles, here worked with different layers of fine fabrics over felt and wadding, with some areas flattened by machine stitching (Penny Lawes)*

18 *This drawing of a dried hosta leaf shows further development in Fig. 39*

idual shapes. Some of these shapes can be sub-divided to suggest different embroidery interpretations, such as those shown in the drawings of the dried hosta leaf.

Shapes can be used to evoke emotions as much as other design elements, for instance, jagged shapes can cause unease whereas smooth shapes might appear tranquil.

Shapes set close together interact and the spaces between are as important as the shapes themselves. One shape on a background reacts with that background and the placing and size need thinking about. Two shapes on a background give many more possibilities:

1 They could be the same size.
2 They could be different sizes.
3 They could be the same size close together.
4 They could be the same size far apart.
5 They could be different sizes close together.
6 They could be different sizes far apart.

From this simple observation, it can be seen that small changes can alter a design completely. There is no hard-and-fast rule, but by developing an awareness and not just accepting the first solution a more satisfactory arrangement may be found.

Plants, trees and flowers are often recognized by their shapes and the way they grow. For instance, are the leaves or flowers rounded or spiky, do they grow upright or do they bend over? A weeping willow is instantly identified by the way it grows. Getting these details of shape correct at the design stage is so much better than trying to put matters right in the middle of a piece of work.

Geometric shapes

Geometric shapes such as the square, circle and the triangle have a sense of order and precision about them which has a great appeal for many embroiderers, the same precision being needed for counted thread embroidery. The variation of pattern from these three shapes can be compared with the variation of music made from eight notes of an octave.

First, consider the circle. It can be thought of as a continuous line enclosing a shape, or as a solid disc, or as a three-dimensional ball. In a group, the circles may all be the same size or differing sizes, like a group of smooth stones. They could be close together, even bumping against each other. They could give a sense of weight and movement, or they could float upwards like bubbles, as light as air.

19 *Circles taken from an Art Nouveau source*

It is thought that the circle was probably one of the first shapes made by man, using a stick to draw in the dust or sand. From this, by sub-dividing and connecting lines, squares were formed until wonderful patterns were created, long before mathematics, as we know it, was thought of.

Pattern

By a combination of line and shape, we arrive at pattern. Pattern may be thought of in two different ways. Arranging a group of objects or shapes can make a pattern which may be pleasing or otherwise, but which is complete in itself. Repeat patterns are another matter altogether. Looking at the wonderful Islamic patterns found on tiles and in architecture, one wonders how on earth anyone could have conceived the ideas. Yet it is interesting that similar patterns are found in ancient civilizations all over the world. The common denominator is a symmetrical motif repeated regularly.

Lewis F. Day, a leading member of the Arts and Crafts Movement in late Victorian England, explained in his book *Pattern Design* his theory of repeating patterns being formed on square or isometric grids. Grids are formed by one series of lines crossing another series of lines at an angle. The grids can be regular square ones as on the usual graph paper, or triangular ones as on isometric graph paper, or they can be irregular and patterns of enormous variety can be formed upon them. Square grids can be made by lines crossing at regular intervals at an angle of 90 degrees. A circle can be made to fit exactly into a square by making the radius half the length of the side of the square, the centre of the circle being where the diagonals of the square cross. This simple unit, if repeated, will form a pattern with a four-sided shape between the circles (see Fig. 20).

If the circles are drawn with a longer radius, the circles will overlap and may be divided further, forming other patterns. As long as they are repeated on the square grid, quite complex arrangements will be made.

Most of us are familiar with the patterns made by pre-formed concrete blocks used to build decorative walls. The individual motif of one block when assembled into a wall can make another pattern. The concrete dividing lines have a thickness and between these thickened pattern lines are holes. If the same idea is used to sub-divide squares, circles and triangles, giving the lines thickness, dramatic patterns form which could be used as a base for cutwork. If the spaces between the thickened lines are thought of as holes, it can be seen how some of the stone tracery found in the medieval cathedrals may have originated.

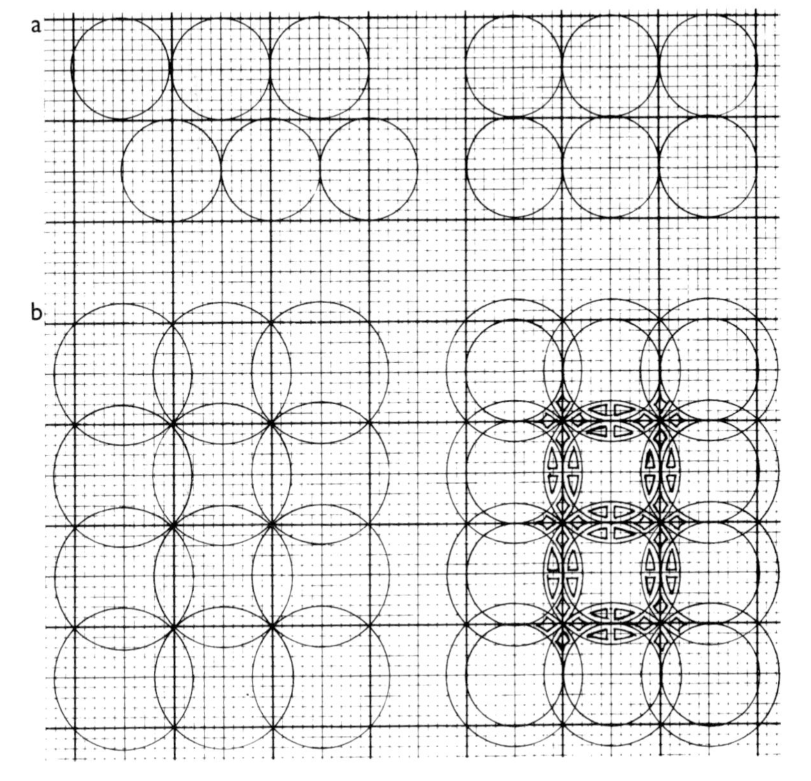

20 *The different shapes which are made between rows of circles when they are placed in different ways on a square grid*
- a *The circle fits the square if it is drawn with the radius equal to half the length of the side of the square*
- b *Larger circles overlapping give scope for complex patterns*

21 a *Some well-known shapes made on a triangular grid*
b *A three-sided shape is made between close-fitting circles on a triangular grid*
c *Patterns made by overlapping circles*

Similarly, regular patterns can be made on isometric grids which are composed of equilateral triangles, that is triangles with all the angles measuring 60 degrees and all the sides the same length. This is the grid on which diamonds and hexagons can be found.

If circles are drawn on this grid, the radius of the circle being half the measurement of a side of the triangle and the centre of the circle being the corner of the triangle, the pattern will be of closely fitting circles with a triangular space between them. If the circles are drawn with a greater radius, the circles will overlap, allowing other patterns to be made.

The triangles, diamonds or hexagons can be sub-divided and, as long as they are repeated regularly on the grid, other patterns will be made. Many patchwork designs can be recognized as coming from these sources. These shapes can

22 *Part of a hanging using organzas and nets over Vilene on a square grid theme (Amanda Clayton)*

23 *A detail of Fig. 22, showing a different-shaped triangle which has a 90 degree angle and two 45 degree angles (Amanda Clayton)*

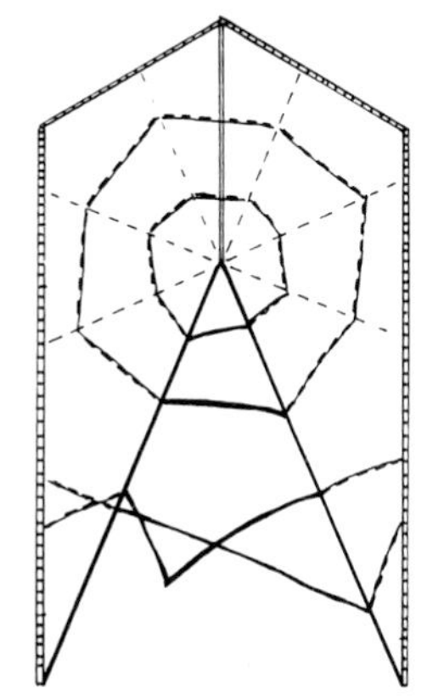

24 *Two mirrors, hinged together and opened to 45 degrees, show a reflected image which fits into a square*

also be used to make stencils or templates to create designs for other techniques such as cutwork or machine embroidery.

Mirrored designs

So far, only divisions of regular geometric shapes, i.e. squares, circles and triangles, have been mentioned. There is another method of making regular patterns which uses two handbag mirrors or, failing this, two mirrored bathroom tiles. Also required is a piece of tracing paper, a really well-sharpened pencil, a ruler and a protractor.

First, make a hinge with a piece of sticky tape to join the two mirrors together. Open the hinge to 90 degrees and stand the mirrors on a pencil scribble. Three reflections and the original will be seen creating a regular motif which would fit into a square. By moving the mirrors around, always keeping the hinge at 90 degrees, many other motifs will be found.

When a pattern has been decided upon, cover the drawing with tracing paper and draw along the two inside edges of the mirrors, marking the area being reflected. Remove the mirrors and trace all the lines within the area. Next, draw a square on a piece of drawing paper and divide it into four equal quarters so that each quarter is big enough to take the tracing. Carefully place the tracing, pencil side down, with

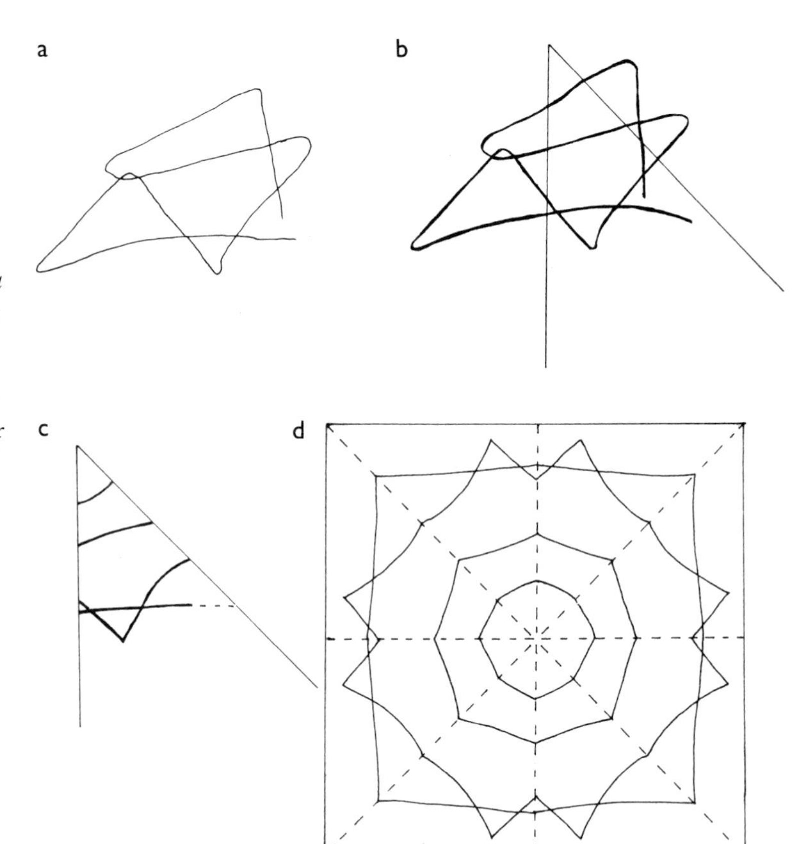

25 *The following sequence shows how a regular pattern can be made from as simple a beginning as a pencil scribble:*
- **a** *The scribble*
- **b** *Placing two hinged mirrors, opened at 45 degrees, on a selected area*
- **c** *A tracing is made and one line, indicated by the dots, is extended*
- **d** *The tracing is transferred to eight equal segments of a square*

the hinge corner to the centre, and draw over the lines of the design. This will transfer the pencil lines beneath onto the drawing paper. When finished, carefully turn the tracing paper over onto the next square and repeat the process, always making sure that the hinge corner is in the centre.

Another way of using this method of design is to change the angle at the hinge of the mirrors. If instead of using 90 degrees, this is halved to 45 degrees, there will be eight sections (seven reflections plus the original) and the design will still fit into a square. Instead of dividing the square on the drawing paper into four parts, eight equal divisions are needed. These are made by drawing diagonal lines from corner to corner. The angle could be divided again into $22\frac{1}{2}$ degrees. Obviously great care and accuracy would be needed for this; it is also why a well-sharpened pencil is required, otherwise the lines when traced become too thick and the definition might be lost.

There are many variations to this technique. Instead of using a pencil scribble, the mirrors could be placed upon a picture in a magazine, or upon pictures of gardens or

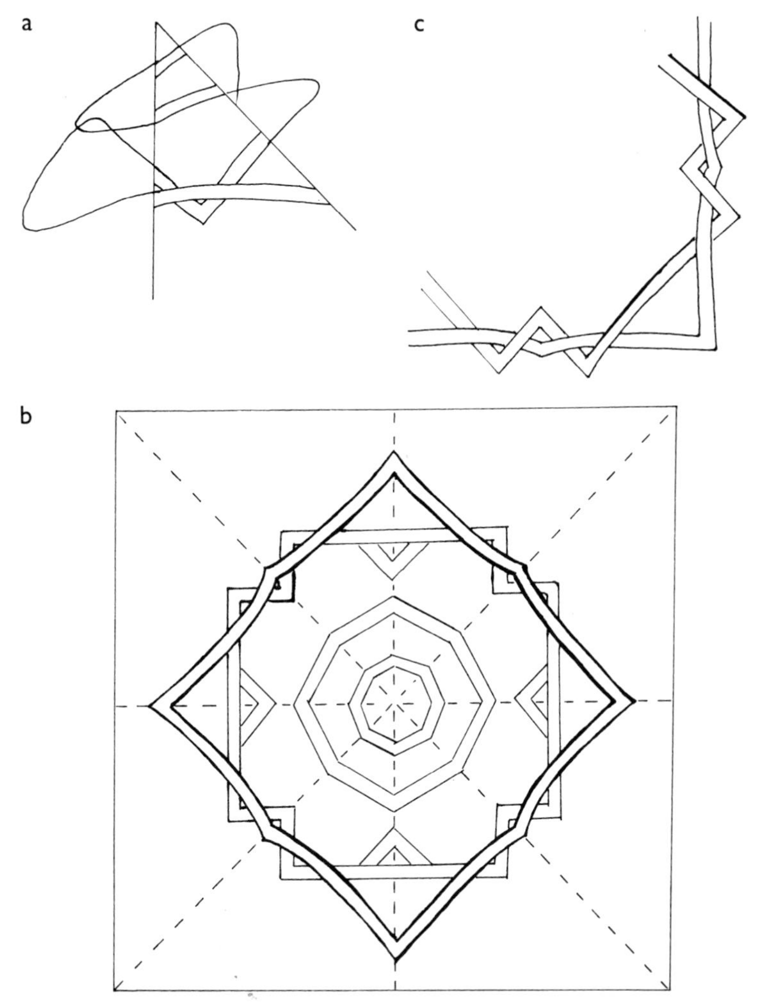

26 a *The same unit as the one used in Fig. 25, but the lines have been thickened*
b *The unit has been transferred to eight equal segments of a square*
c *By making a few alterations, some lines could be made to interlace*

flowers. Another interesting, and sometimes very surprising, result comes from placing the mirrors upon a piece of embroidery.

This design method can be useful in deciding a colour scheme. For instance, when all four corners have been drawn, if each one is coloured differently the mirrors can be placed to reflect each square so that the complete design can be seen in each colour.

So far, the measurements for the angle at the hinge give a design which fits into a square. If 60, 30 or 15 degree angles are used, these will create designs which fit into hexagons.

These symmetrical motifs can be used by themselves as an individual design, or repeated on a regular square or isometric grid.

Grids do not have to be regular. They can be made by lines joining irregular divisions, which leads to exciting

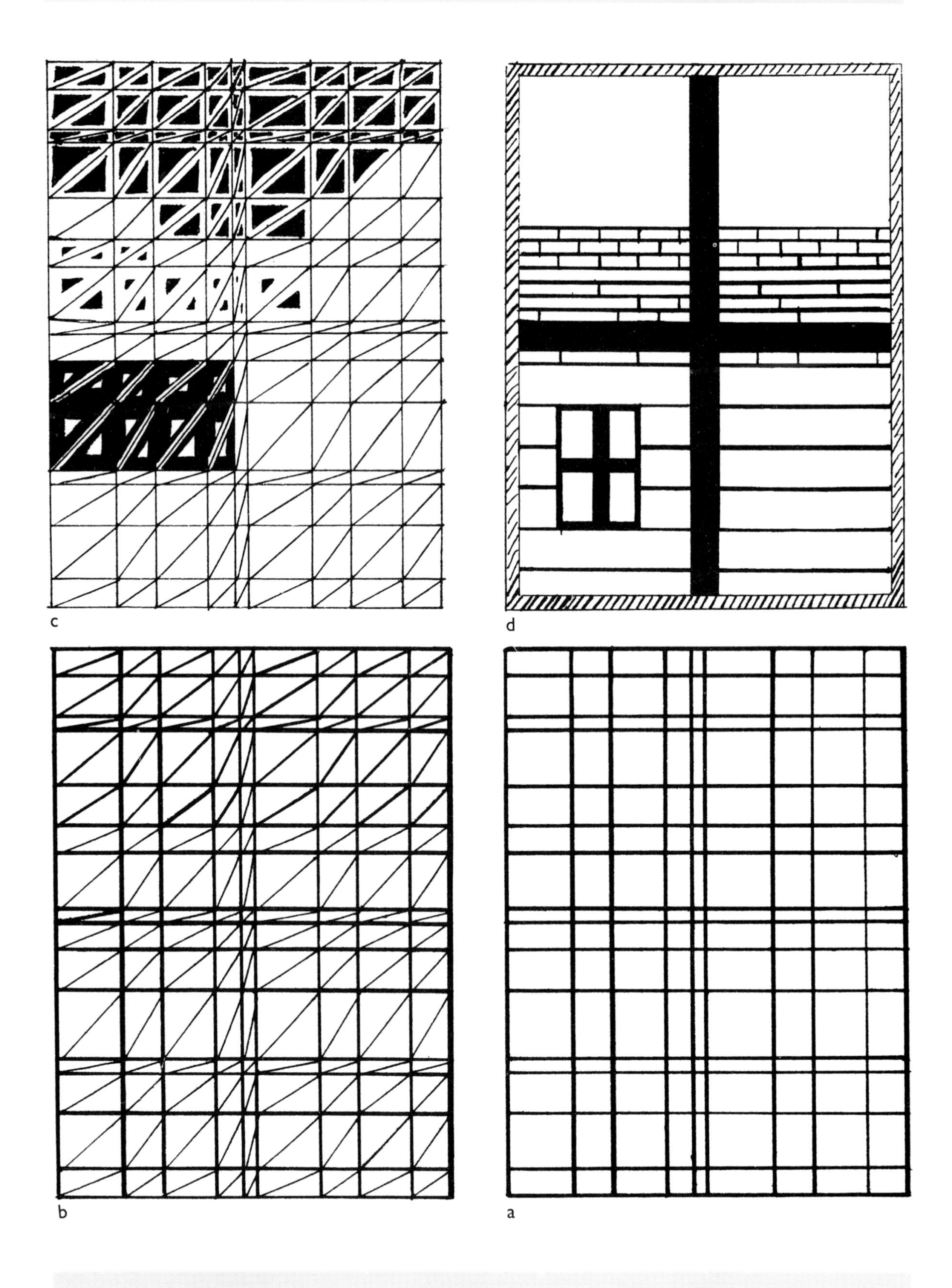
c
d
b
a

28 *Another grid can be made by using random measurements along all four sides of a rectangle*

patterns and, at times, strange optical effects. They can be seen all around us, for example, in tower blocks, scaffolding and simple brickwork. In a walled garden with a grid of supporting wires, there is a double grid; wire netting forms yet another grid. All these can be useful starting points for design.

If an overhead projector or an enlarging photocopying machine is available, the scale of these patterns can be enlarged, giving a completely new appearance. Different-scale designs need different treatments, and this allows individuals to follow their own preferences, to work a tiny, intricate piece of embroidery or to carry out a much larger piece with folded or pleated fabrics. The proportions might be the same, but the final pieces would be vastly different.

Colour

Colour is very personal. One person prefers strong, vibrant colours, while another prefers pale, subtle ones. Colour is known to change mood, and has even been proved to alter a person's temperature.

Colour is such an enormous subject in its own right that it is impossible to discuss it in depth in this book. On the other hand, it is such an important element of design that a few guidelines might be found useful and lead the reader to further studies and experiments.

The primary colours, red, blue and yellow, cannot be made by mixing other colours together. However, this does not mean that there is only one red, one blue or one yellow. In fact, it is very difficult, if not impossible, to find a completely neutral red, that is a red without a leaning either

27 a *A grid made on graph paper from random measurements*
b *The shapes made are each divided by a diagonal line, making a more complex grid*
c *Different treatments are made to the shapes, which could be interpreted in cutwork, reverse appliqué or appliqué*
d *Grids found within grids*

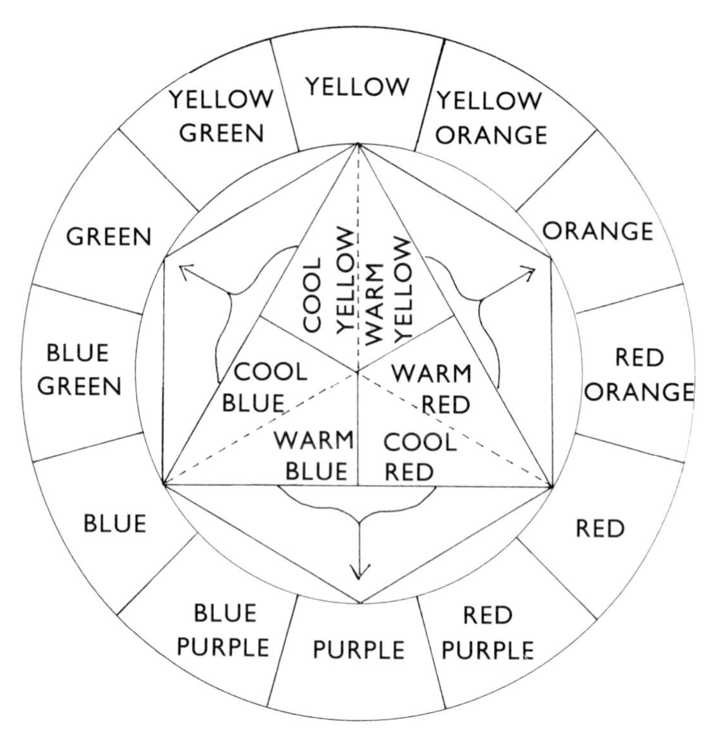

29 *A colour wheel, showing how the different primary colours might be mixed to make true secondary colours*

towards orange or purple. This is why in Chapter 5 it is stressed that two reds, two blues and two yellows are required in order to mix other colours.

Colours are often described as warm or cold, for instance, red is thought of as warm and blue as cold, but each primary colour can be thought of as having a warm and a cold version depending on what it is next to. An orange-red such as vermilion is considered a warm red; next to it, crimson, which is a blue-red, could be thought cold, or at least cool. Ultramarine blue is a warm blue, whereas Prussian blue, which is a slightly green-blue, is cold. Even yellow has a warm and a cold side, lemon yellow being cooler than egg yolk yellow.

These differences are particularly important when it comes to mixing colours, especially with so many embroiderers now wishing to use fabric paints and dyes. Without doubt, the best way to understand colour is to mix it. Most people know that by mixing two primaries together a secondary colour is made. Thus, by mixing red and blue the result should be purple. The word 'should' has been used deliberately, since if the red used is an orange-red, the result will be more brown than purple – a good colour, but not purple. From Fig. 00, it will be seen that the primary colours nearest to the secondary colours being mixed are the ones to use.

Many, many colours can be mixed from these primaries and secondaries, including toning down a strong colour by adding a little of its complementary. All colours can be made paler by adding white, or water according to the paint being used, so that from red a whole range to palest pink can be mixed. Equally, by adding black, colours can be darkened to rich jewel-like colours. By adding greys, from palest to charcoal grey, a range of subtle, moody colours can be created.

Colour is of particular importance when you are using transparent fabrics. One colour placed over another does not act like paint, but it can change the tones of the threads and fabrics underneath to a considerable degree. Almost more important is the difference made by putting the colour behind a piece of work when it is mounted, which acts in a similar way to a painter putting a glaze over a painting.

Embroiderers usually work with already-coloured fabrics and threads, but even with these, other colours can appear to be made by using the 'pointillist' method of putting small amounts of colour together and letting the eye do the mixing. Here again, it is necessary to use the correct reds and blues if you wish them to merge into purple. Colours close together on the colour wheel blend together well and are harmonious. If a bit of excitement is needed, a colour from the opposite side of the colour wheel, the complementary colour, may be the answer. Proportion is essential to all elements of design, and this is particularly so when dealing with colour; too many coloured threads mixed together will act in the same way as mixing many colours of paint, a muddy result.

An interesting exercise would be to collect unusual colours from colour magazines and brochures, stick them in a sketchbook and then try to simulate the colours (1) using paint, (2) sticking down small pieces of threads, paper and transparent fabrics. Using the same unusual colours, find the complementary colour and different tones of the complementary colour, to judge how these affect the original (tone being the lightness or darkness of a colour). Finally, simulate the same unusual colours by overlapping and pleating small pieces of transparent fabric and stitching over them so that the stitches and the background create a rich texture of the colour.

Confidence in the use of colour comes with understanding, which comes with practice and experiment.

CHAPTER **2**

Shadow techniques

Shadow work

One type of embroidery always associated with transparent fabrics is shadow work. It was popular during the eighteenth century for decorating christening and bridal gowns, and continued to be used into this century for the decoration of pillowcases, tableware and lingerie. In the 1930s, the Needlework Development Scheme issued a pamphlet showing how shadow work could be used to decorate lingerie.

Basically, shadow work uses a fine fabric such as cotton organdie, silk organza, muslin or fine silk, stitched either on the wrong side of the fabric using closed herringbone stitch, or on the right side of the fabric using double back stitch. In either case, this means that the outline of the shape is seen on the right side of the fabric, and the shadow of the stitch fills the shape.

Design

When designing for this technique, shapes should be kept simple and not too wide, otherwise the stitch is too long and becomes slack. If a wide shape is required, the problem can be solved by careful dividing. A choice must be made whether to work two separate areas, which means either a double line of surface stitches, or to work the second shape into the stitches of the first. Whichever choice is made, the decision should enhance the design.

Linear qualities are important in shadow work as the outlining stitch is seen on the right side, and the thread

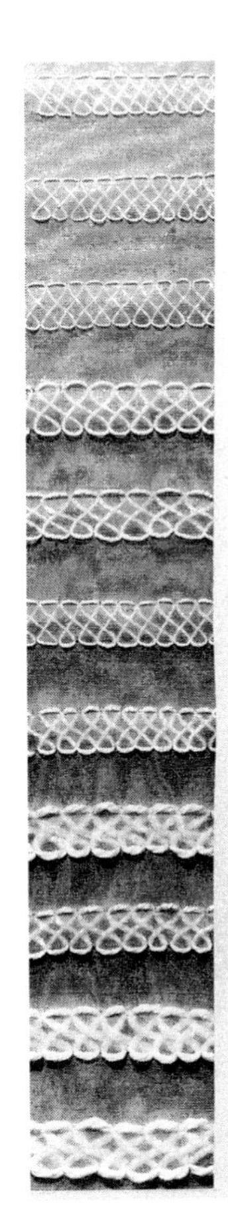

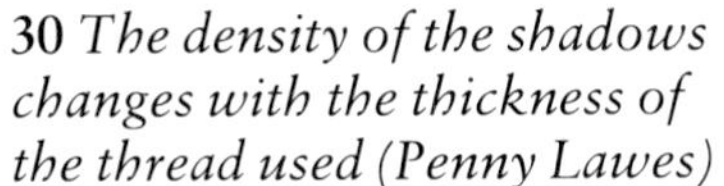

30 *The density of the shadows changes with the thickness of the thread used (Penny Lawes)*

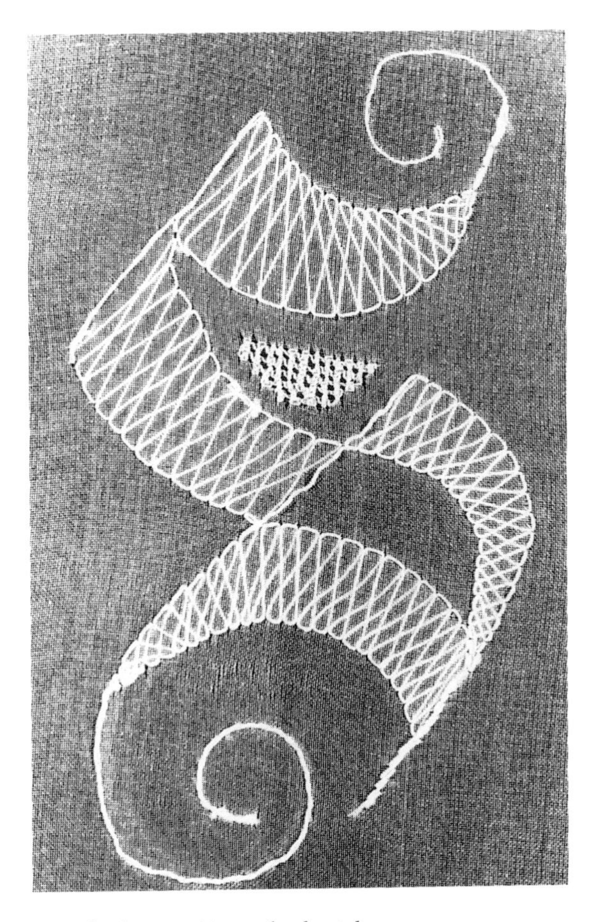

31 *The letter 'S' worked with fine white thread on silk organza*

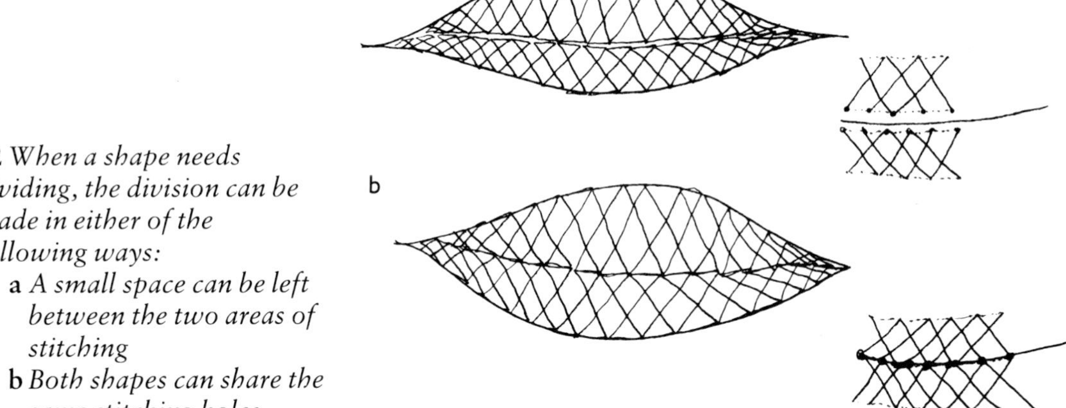

32 *When a shape needs dividing, the division can be made in either of the following ways:*

- **a** *A small space can be left between the two areas of stitching*
- **b** *Both shapes can share the same stitching holes*

appears much brighter than its shadow crossing the shape on the reverse side.

This embroidery technique is particularly suitable for designs with stripes or narrow shapes, and for linear designs such as those found in:

1 Art Nouveau designs
2 animal markings, such as cats, tigers or zebras
3 strata in rock formations
4 trees and plants
5 shells

These subjects can be developed further by taking sections and repeating them on a grid to create other patterns.

Transferring the design

As the fabric is transparent, the design can be traced directly onto it. Normally it is not advisable to use a graphite pencil on fabric as it makes the sewing thread look dirty, but a hard

33 *The letter is worked in the manner of an illuminated manuscript. The main shapes were dyed a deep blue and stitched, using closed herringbone stitch on silk organza. The decorative scrolls were worked in pin stitch in reds and greens. Small pieces of gold purl were added to the end shapes*

pencil such as a 3H or 4H with a fine point should not mark. Alternatively, a very well-sharpened watercolour pencil, choosing the same colour as the thread to be used, is suitable and easy to apply.

If you are using closed herringbone stitch and working on the wrong side of the fabric, the design will be seen more clearly if it is traced onto the wrong side. If you are using double back stitch, the design can be traced onto the right side. A word of warning is needed here: if you are tracing onto the wrong side, remember that the design needs to be reversed.

If you are tracing from a pencilled drawing, there is a danger that graphite from the drawing may be transferred to the fabric, which again may discolour the sewing thread. To avoid this, the design should be placed under a sheet of plastic or in a plastic folder, and the fabric held securely on top; the design can then be traced without the problem of marking the fabric.

Working methods

Although the fabric is usually fine, the same maxim applies as to most other embroidery techniques – the needle should make way for the thread to follow. If a fine thread is being used a fine needle (usually a crewel) is suitable, but if a thicker thread is chosen a larger-size needle should be used to prevent the sewing thread rubbing against the threads of the fabric.

With all transparent fabrics, beginnings and finishings need care in order not to look bulky and obtrusive. Rather than starting with a back stitch or a knot, it is usually better to leave a tail of thread about 10 cm (4 in) long to return to at the end of sewing, threading the needle with this tail and finishing off with a tiny back stitch behind a stitch.

Closed herringbone stitch is worked from left to right, remembering that the thread emerges from a hole shared with the previous stitch and that the threads cross twice and interlace. The lines outlining the shape are worked as shown in Fig. 34.

Working from a closed corner may seem more difficult, but if the same instruction is followed the shape will be enclosed on the right side.

If a curve is more pronounced on one side than the other, the stitches on the curve will need to be a little bit wider to keep a regular look.

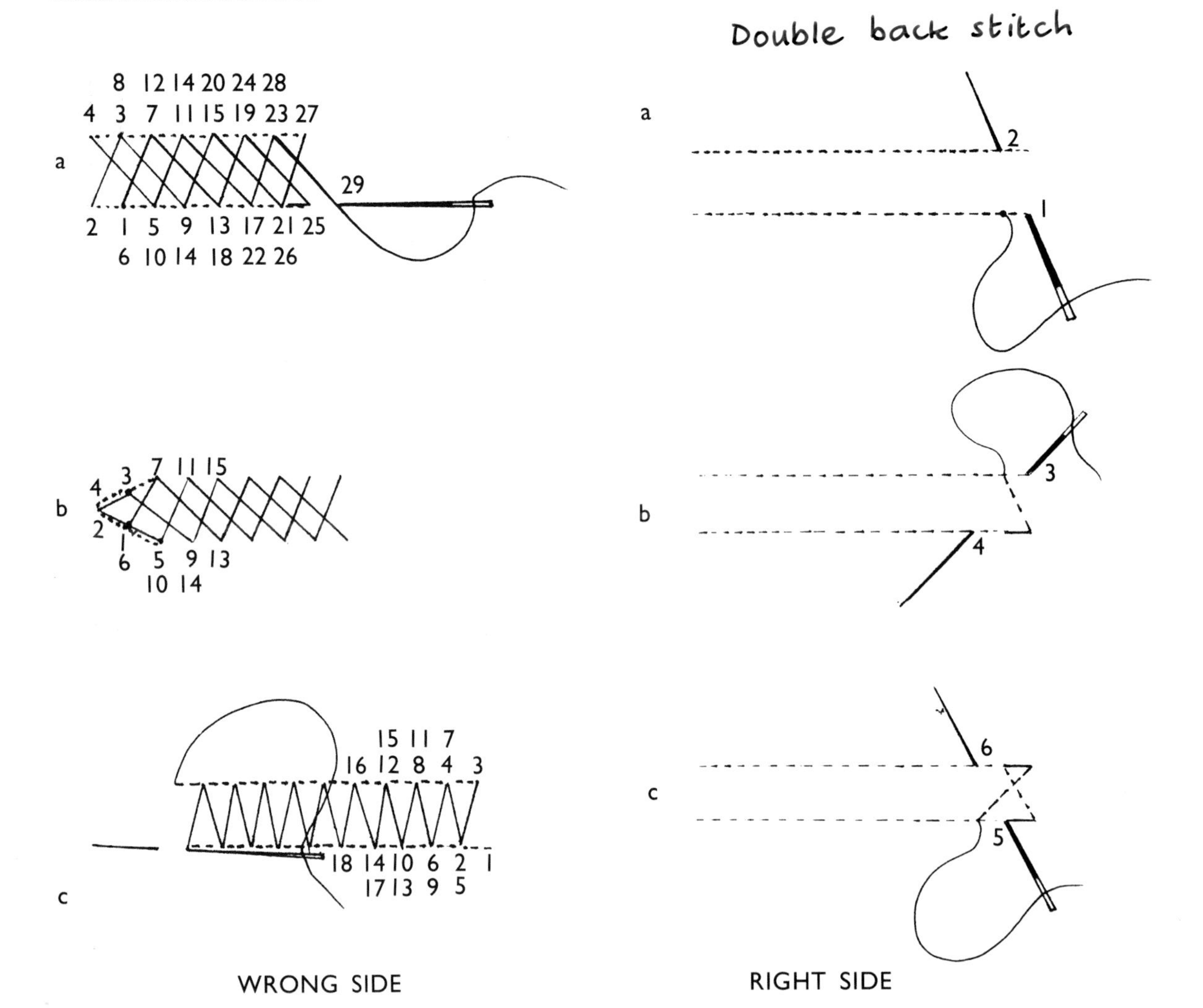

34 *Working closed herringbone stitch:*
- a *The needle enters the fabric at the odd numbers and emerges from the fabric at the even numbers*
- b *To close a point, the same sequence of stitching should be followed*
- c *The stitch used for Indian shadow work is a zigzag, starting at the right-hand side and working towards the left. It is worked on the wrong side*

When a shape has one closed end and one open end, the open end can be finished off with a line of back stitches (see Fig. 00).

Double back stitch is worked on the right side of the fabric from right to left, and gives exactly the same result as closed herringbone. Using double back stitch sometimes makes it easier to keep a regular stitch and outline. Start with a back stitch, leaving a tail of thread to fasten off with at the end.

By slightly pulling the working thread, the shape can be given a raised look. This applies only if the shape is enclosed, and it is better to work in the hand rather than in a frame.

A variation of the usual shadow work, known as Indian shadow work, looks the same on the right side, but the threads do not cross on the wrong side. It is worked from

35 *Double back stitch looks exactly the same as closed herringbone stitch, but it is worked on the right side of the fabric, stitching from right to left. The needle should enter the fabric on the odd numbers and emerge on the even numbers*

right to left and, to maintain a good shadow effect, only a small amount of fabric is picked up for each stitch. The stitch forms a zigzag on the wrong side.

Shadow work can be worked with white thread on a suitable white fabric. White on white is satisfactory and pleasing, particularly if different thicknesses of thread are used to give different densities of shadow. Colours can also be used to great effect, both fabrics and threads. Black thread with white fabric gives a good shadow, but it must be remembered that the black outline stitch on the surface will give a strong contrast.

Variations

1 Apart from using coloured threads, colour may be added by cutting out the shape in a coloured transparent fabric (preferably one which does not fray easily, such as silk organza) and placing this on the wrong side, holding it in place with the herringbone stitch.

36 a, b, c *The zebra is a suitable subject for shadow work, either as the complete animal or, by selecting an area to repeat, a design could be made using mirror images, as described in Chapter 1*

2 Instead of using coloured fabric, dye could be used to colour the shape before stitching (see Chapter 5).
3 Two or three layers could be worked and placed one over another to create depth or mistiness.
4 Herringbone stitch might be worked alternately on top and underneath.
5 The outline could be worked in straight stitch on the machine, and the stitches laced on the wrong side.

Shadow quilting

Another shadow technique, shadow quilting uses fabric to create the shadow and shows the design in relief. A strong-coloured filling is sandwiched between two layers of fabric, both of which may be transparent or just the top layer. The shapes are then stitched round, using back stitch.

As well as being a strong colour, the padding material should not fray, so for these reasons felt is a very suitable choice. One fabric to avoid is velvet, which sheds its pile and is difficult to control. If velvet is particularly wanted, it could be backed with an iron-on stiffener.

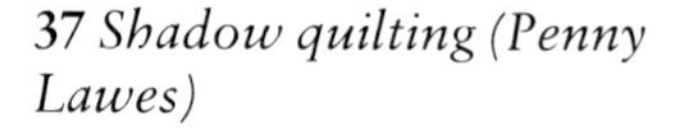

37 *Shadow quilting (Penny Lawes)*

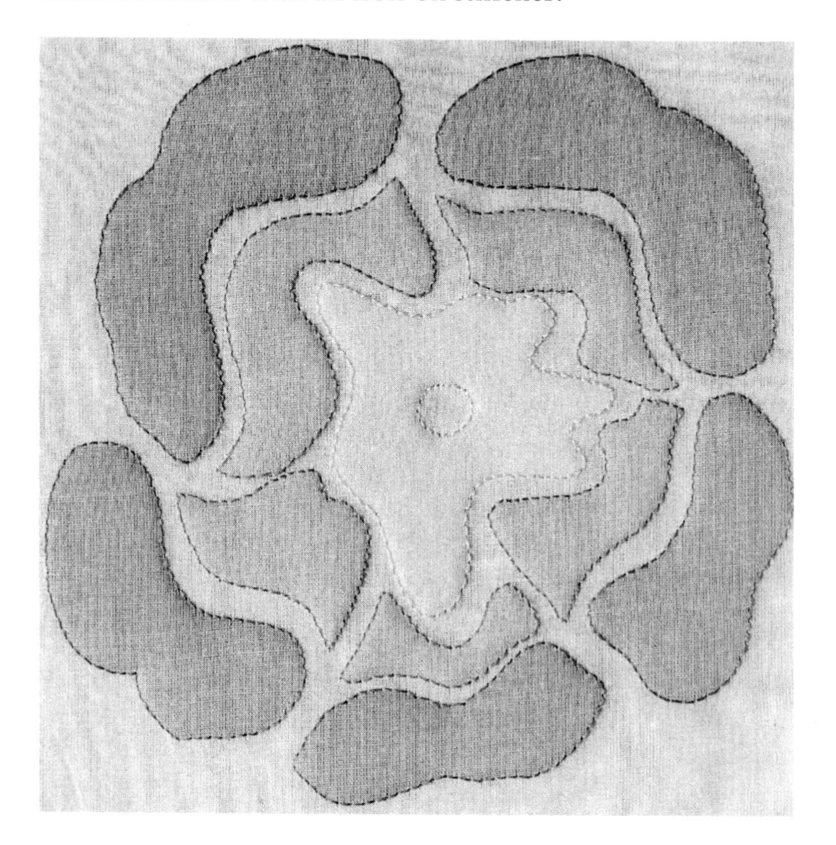

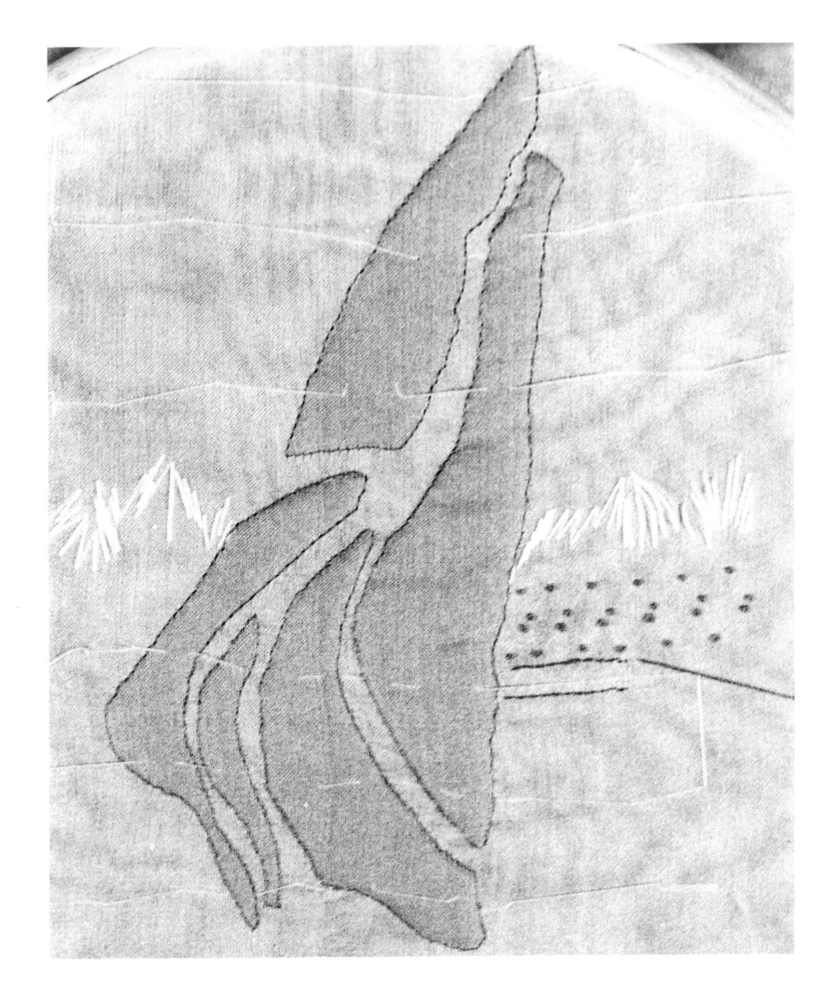

38 *The design is taken from a dried hosta leaf. The sample shows the layers of materials held together with tacking stitches to prevent movement during stitching*

Design

The design should consist of simple shapes which relate well to each other. Fig. 38 shows a leaf which has been cut into segments, leaving spaces between for the stitching. In this case, the design is more satisfactory if the shapes are not all the same size; the spaces between can also vary. If the design is a geometric one, then a more regular approach may be needed. In all cases, sufficient space must be left for the stitching, which sometimes means two rows quite close together.

Method

If the background fabric is transparent, place it over the design. Position the felt pieces on top, checking that there is enough room between the shapes for stitching, and tack them in position. Take care that no knots are on the surface,

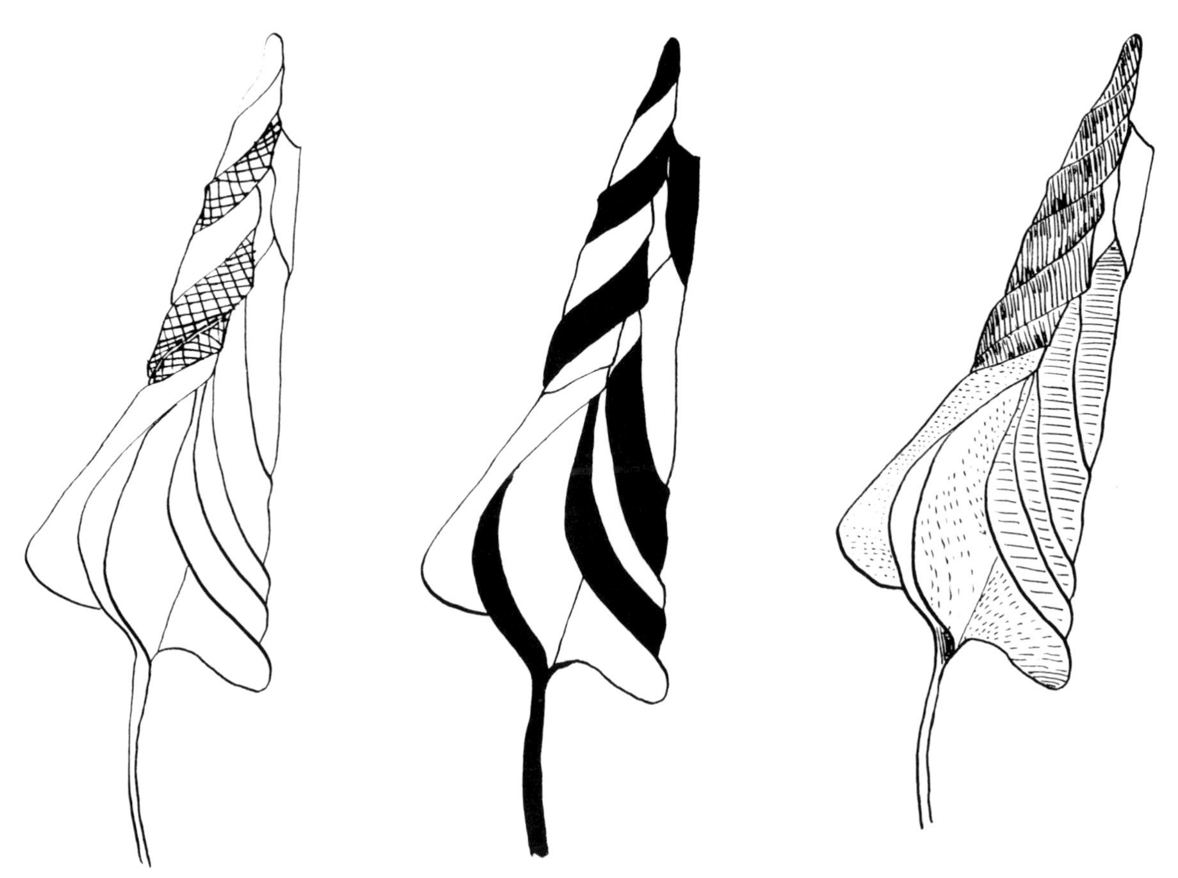

39 *Developments of the hosta leaf theme*

where they might be trapped. Place the top layer of transparent fabric on top and tack through all layers. This preparation is important if the layers are not to slip during stitching.

Back stitch round the shapes, choosing either the fabric colour or the now muted colour of the padding.

Corded or Italian quilting

This type of quilting can also be worked using transparent fabric for the top layer. If the quilting wool is coloured or dyed, it will show through as muted colour.

Design

A good source of design for this technique, which will consist of parallel lines, can be found among the intricate interlacing patterns of Celtic origin. Art Nouveau, with its curving sinuous lines, is another rich area to investigate. It is well worth drawing the design in a double line in order to

40 *A butterfly worked with shadow quilting and surface stitchery (Dorothy McCulloch)*

41 *Italian shadow quilting, showing the wool in the channels (Penny Lawes)*

42 *A combination of shadow work, corded quilting, hand and machine stitching have been used to interpret this design, called 'White Face' (Gill Thompson)*

determine where one line crosses another. Quite small areas of double lines repeated regularly within triangles or squares can create formal patterns, used for herb gardens or borders.

Method

Trace the design onto the transparent fabric, using a well-sharpened watercolour pencil. Place this over the backing fabric and tack them together. The stitching may be worked by hand, using back stitch, or on the machine. When the lines of stitching are completed, coloured quilting wool is threaded through the channels from the back.

Shadow trapunto quilting

This method of quilting may also be used with transparent fabrics. Mark out the design on the transparent material and place it on top of the backing fabric. The two layers are held together with tacking stitches round the edges. Back stitch or machine the chosen shapes, making sure they are completely enclosed. A small slit can then be made in the background fabric, through which to push the chosen filling – small pieces of folded fabrics, or a mixture of wool and silk threads cut into small lengths, or even small beads. To finish, oversew the slits in the back.

CHAPTER **3**

Appliqué

Appliqué is a term which is generally used to mean the addition of one fabric to the surface of another one to form a design.

When using transparent materials, certain considerations need to be taken into account. According to the purpose of the finished piece of work, there will be times when hems need to be turned and these will show through as a more opaque edge. This can be exploited as part of the design, but it should be thought of at the design stage.

In the past, transparent fabrics were thought of as delicate and, of course, that was, and still is, a great part of their charm. Today we can enjoy this same delicacy and charm coupled with the strength and easy care of fine synthetic materials. With this advantage, we are able once again to consider beautiful tablemats or clothes or fine curtains without having to spend hours with an iron.

Method I

First, let us look at a traditional way of applying by hand a fine piece of fabric, a method as valid today as it ever was.

The shape to be applied should not be too complicated. When cutting out, make sure that the grain of the applied piece matches that of the bottom layer of fabric, and allow $\frac{1}{2}$ cm ($\frac{1}{4}$ in) for turnings. Tack the piece in place, slightly more than 1 cm ($\frac{1}{2}$ in) in from the cut edge; this will leave room for a $\frac{1}{2}$ cm ($\frac{1}{4}$ in) hem to be turned under and stitched in place. Where the design has an outward curve, snip out

43 a *Appliqué. Tack the fabric to be applied in position along the lines marked –a–. Cut notches from the outer edge, turn under at line –b–, and slip stitch or pin stitch*

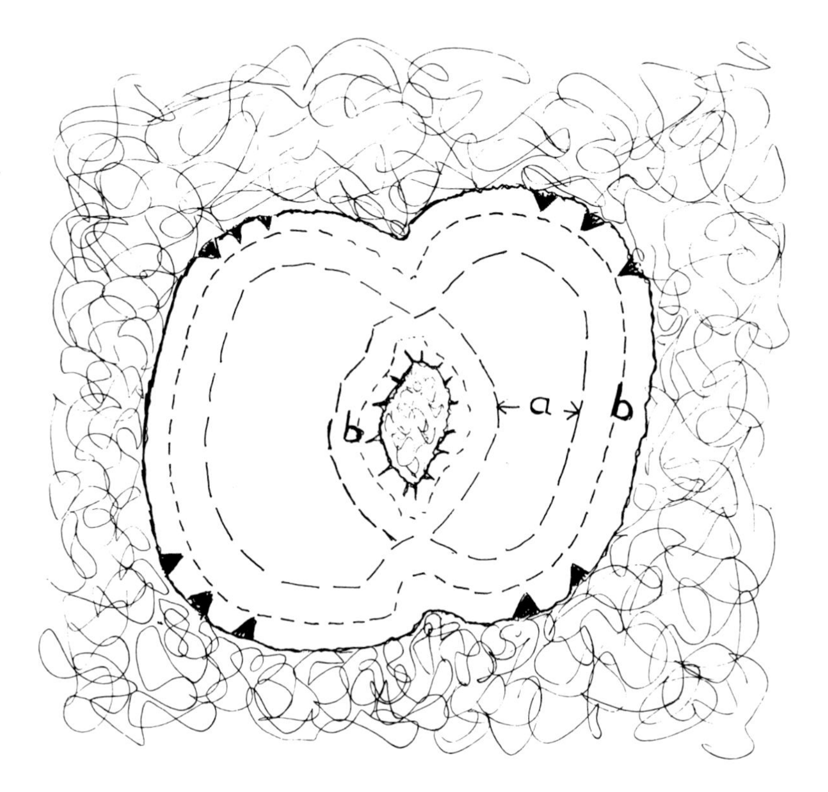

b *The applied piece pin stitched in position*

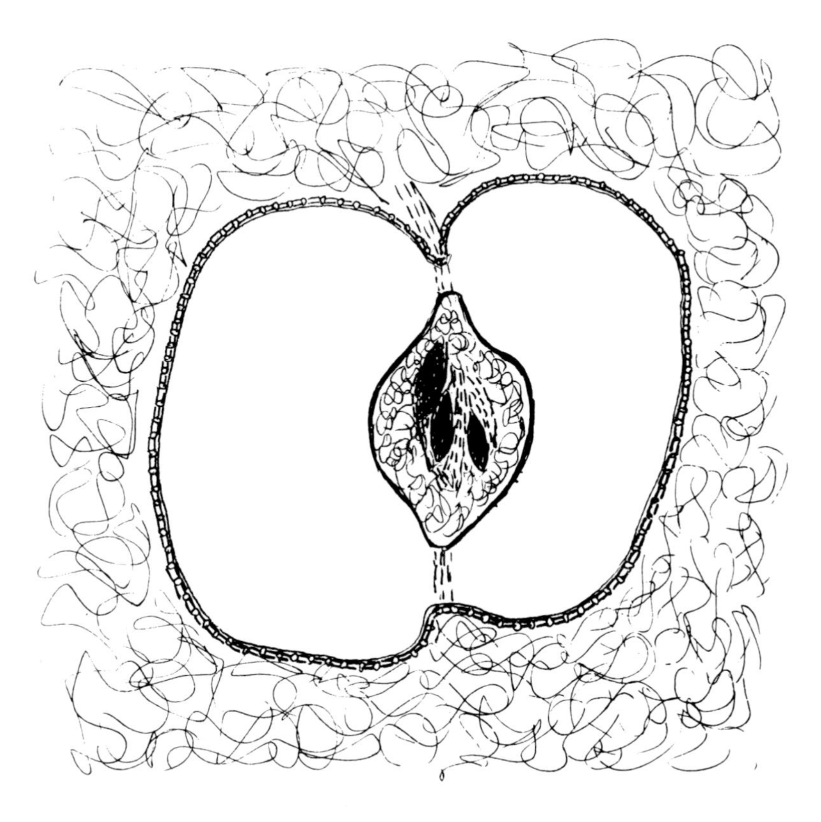

small triangles, almost up to the $\frac{1}{2}$ cm ($\frac{1}{4}$ in) fold line; where there is an inward curve, simply make small snips.

Turn under the hem a little bit at a time and slip stitch down, using a fine matching thread and a fine needle. Pin stitch would give a more pronounced and decorative edge. This may be sufficient or an alternative could be a parallel line of running stitches, inside the folded edge.

Method 2 Pin stitch

Pin stitch can be used as a pulled work stitch or as a hem stitch, and is a practical stitch to use with transparent fabric needing a hem. It can also be used where a hem is not needed but where a small piece of fabric is to be applied, as on a panel. In this case, draw the design on the fabric to be applied, using a well-sharpened watercolour pencil. Do not

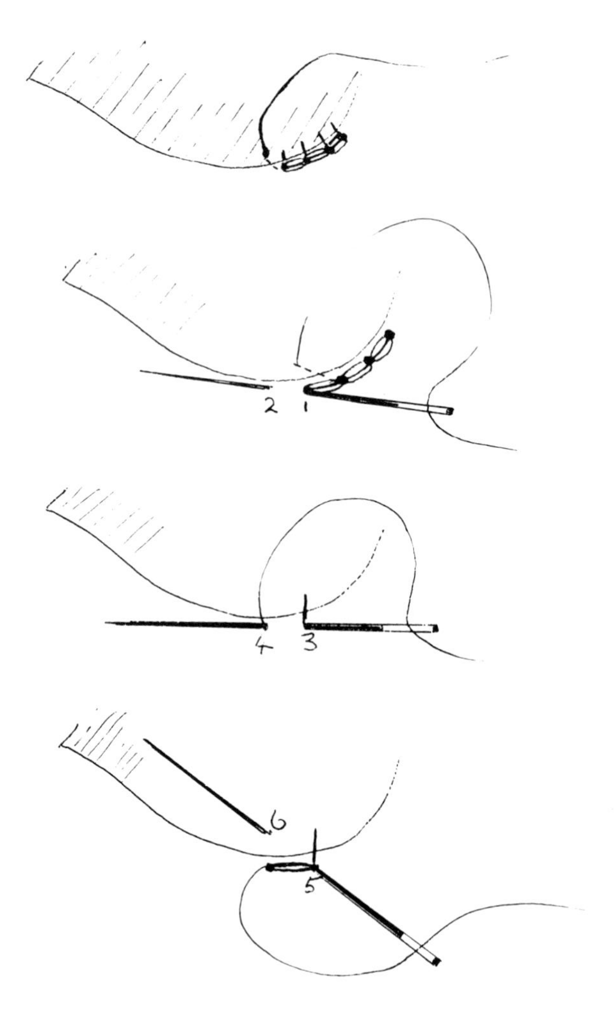

44 *The three phases of working pin stitch. Each time, the needle enters the fabric on the odd number and emerges on the even number*

cut out the shape, but tack it in place and pin stitch along the marked outline. When finished, cut away the surplus material. As mentioned earlier, begin by leaving about 10 cm (4 in) of thread, returning to this at the end to fasten off.

Pin stitch enables quite sensitive curves to be made, where this is required. Although it needs care, it is an easy stitch, and if a little time is given to practise it, the reward will repay the effort. It is really two back stitches worked into the same holes, with the second back stitch finished by bringing the needle through just above the last hole, ready to start the next stitch.

45 *How to apply without a hem. Mark the piece to be applied with the finished shape and tack in position. Pin stitch round the required shape, then cut away the excess fabric*

Shadow appliqué

Another method which is very practical, since all raw edges are enclosed, is shadow appliqué. In theory, this is the same as shadow quilting, but instead of the enclosed pieces being padded they are flat and flexible. As a consequence, this method is suitable for tableware or as decoration for clothes. Suitable designs could be taken from flowers, fruit,

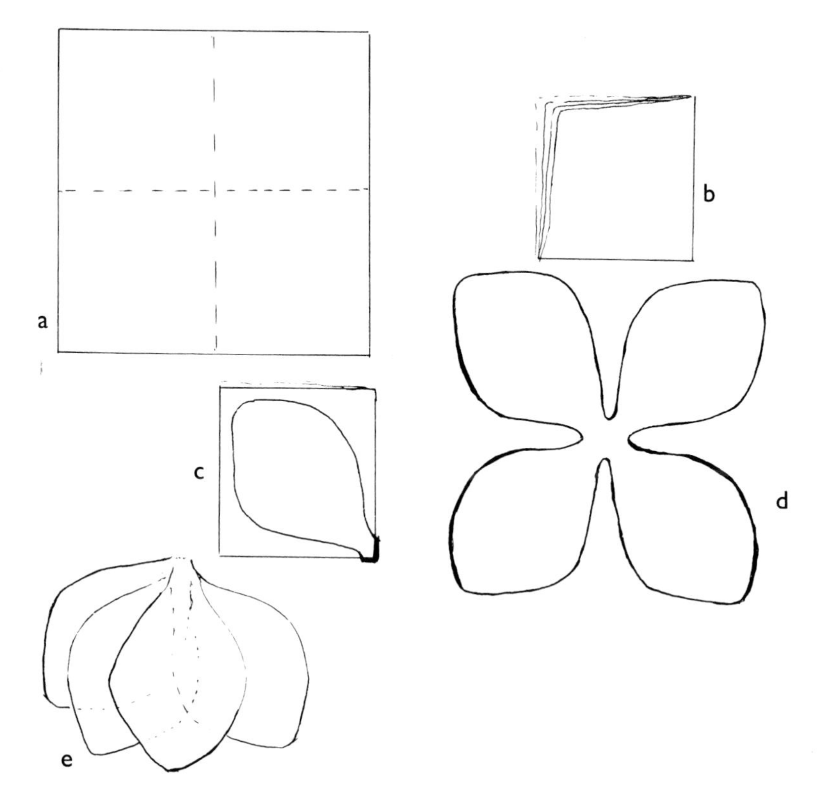

46 *Cutting the petals for the cyclamen flowers. Because the fabric is fine, it can be folded over itself quite easily. This is much easier to handle than coping with individual pieces*
- **a** *Fold the square along the dotted lines*
- **b** *The folded square*
- **c** *Cut out the petal shape, making sure not to cut at the corner*
- **d** *The petal shape opened out*
- **e** *Fold the petals over each other. Being transparent, where they overlap the colour is deeper*

leaves, geometric sources or letters. If you are using a flower design, such as the cyclamen in Fig. 46, it is much easier if the petals are cut as one. Fold the fabric in four and cut out a petal shape, making sure that the petals are left joined together in one corner, rather as children fold paper to make snowflakes or paper dolls.

Because the fabric is fine, the petals can be folded over and rearranged to resemble the cyclamen. Where the petals cross each other, the transparent fabric will create deeper tones.

The flower can now be tacked in place on the bottom layer of fabric, taking care there are no knots on the surface which could become trapped between the layers.

On the surface layer, decide where the leaves are to be and work the beautiful markings of the cyclamen leaves in the shadow work technique of closed herringbone stitch on the underside (see p. 38). Cut the leaf shape from a suitable material and place it behind the stitched outline, then tack in place. The bottom and the top layers of fabric can now be tacked together, with the flower shapes and the leaves sandwiched in between. This tacking is important if the various layers of materials are to stay in place during the stitching.

47 *The cyclamen has one of its leaves not backed by a fabric. The marking of the leaf is worked in very uneven herringbone stitch. The bottom left leaf is shown with the leaf shape tacked in place, but not yet stitched*

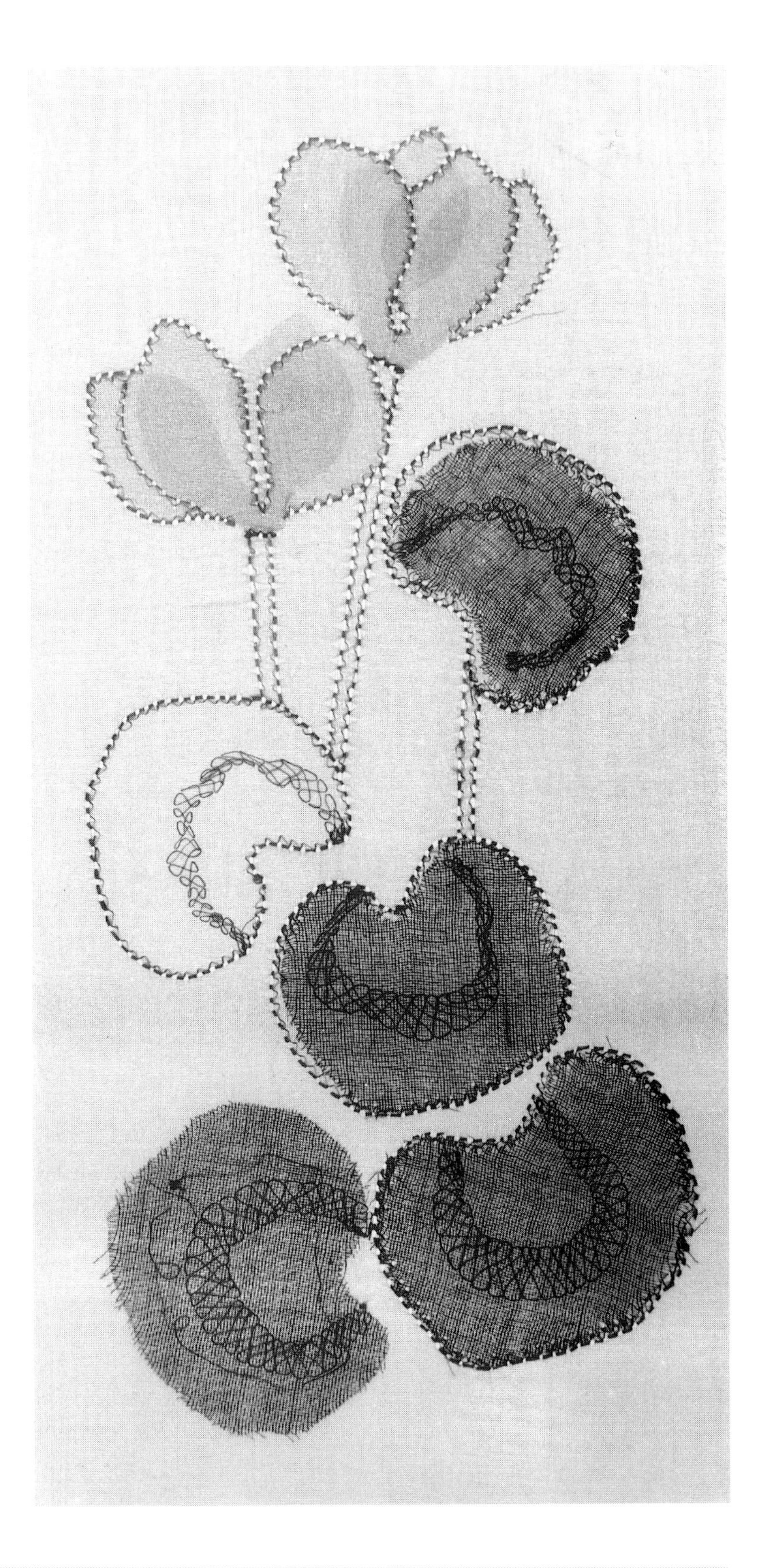

Choose an easy place to start stitching, not a corner or an intricate area. Using pin stitch, outline the flower or leaf shape so that the back stitch lies at the edge of the shapes and the little down stroke goes through the applied piece. Stems and other 'drawing lines' can also be worked in pin stitch. An alternative to pin stitch could be another pulled stitch, three-sided stitch.

Turning under the edges of fine fabrics is quite a tricky operation, particularly for such things as bias binding. There is on the market, available in haberdashery departments, a simple gadget for making bias binding, which turns the edges under automatically as you draw through a strip

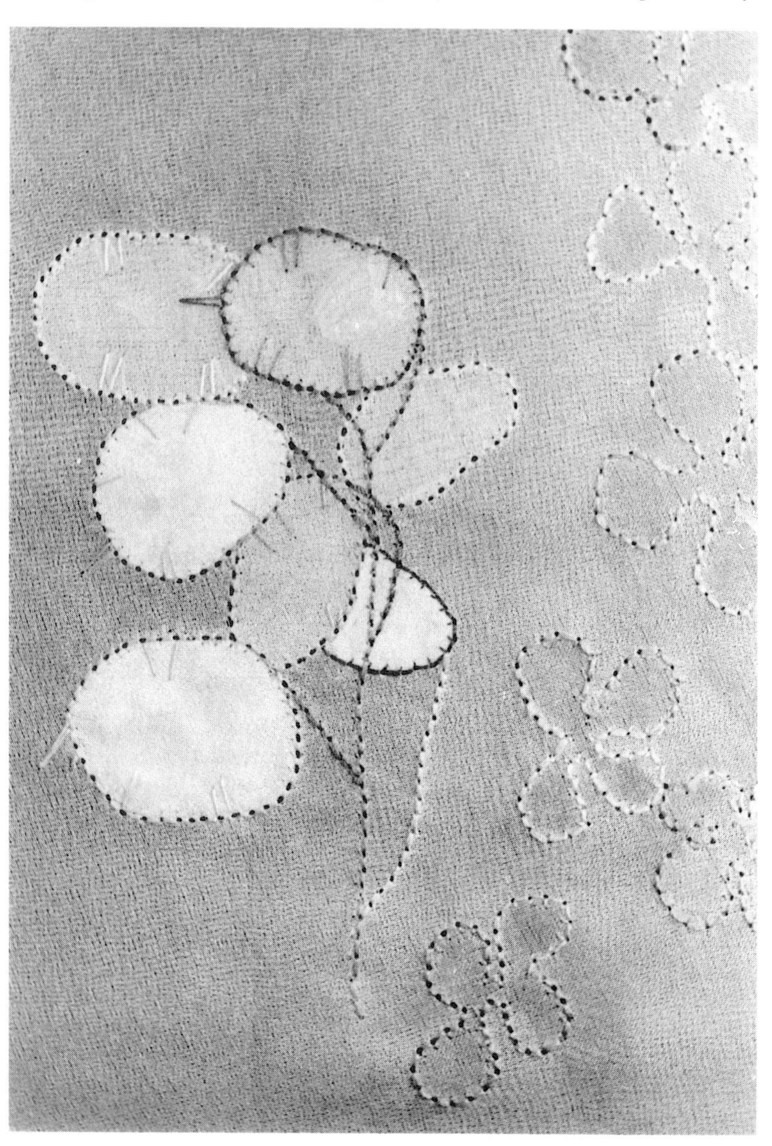

48 *Honesty seed pods, using shadow appliqué*

of the fabric. The material can be cut on the straight grain as well as on the bias. If the narrow resin web used for turning up hems is fed in with the strip of material, the binding can be stiffened. (It is advisable to protect the iron and ironing board by placing silicone paper, such as that used in baking, on both sides of the fabric when you iron it.) These strips can then be applied by hand or machine to create a pattern, used on panels as fences or window frames, or woven into grids.

Design for appliqué

Leaving the practical side of appliqué and turning to the more creative use of attaching one fabric to another, it is now possible to exploit some of the properties of these delicate fabrics. One of the delights of the coloured organzas is to overlap one over another, changing both the tone and the density. Landscapes can be made by overlapping different irregular-width strips, creating the impression of fields and hedges, distant hills and skies. It is worth spending time at this stage to make sure that proportions, colours and the general atmosphere are correct for the desired effect; it is easier to make changes at this stage than later, when the stitching is under way.

Keep the colours and the stitches flatter and quieter and smaller in the distance, starting from the back and working forwards and bringing more warmth and texture into the foreground. This is only a very general guide, and the fabrics chosen as the base will play an important part in the finished work.

Developing an idea

In the piece of work based on spring bulbs (Fig. 49), the first phase was to use pastels to put down on paper the blocks of colour relating to the bulbs. This was the first move away from the precise picture of the flowers. Using a finger, the pastels were gently rubbed to make a blurred image, and from this drawing corresponding areas of coloured organzas were cut out and tacked down on a background. The colour of the background fabric was important: a dark colour was chosen to give richness when the organzas were placed on top, thereby keeping the vibrant effect of the bulbs. The surface stitching was worked mainly to enhance the colours and merge the fabrics together.

49 *A progression of ideas, starting with a picture of spring bulbs:*
a *Spring bulbs*
b *Dividing the bulbs into blocks of colour*
c *Drawing in blocks of stitches*

This method of moving from a representational to a more abstract design is a useful one and very easy to do. It is surprising how quickly ideas for embroidery are suggested. Using fine coloured fabrics in this way creates a good balance between fabric and thread without the final piece being overworked.

From a photograph, a drawing of a spray of leaves, or even working directly from a plant, a simple design for appliqué can be made using transparent fabrics, exploiting the fact that in sunlight one leaf is seen behind another. Trace the chosen leaf and cut out a template in either stiff paper or thin card, then use the template to mark and cut out a number of leaves in paper. Use these to work out a design, looking carefully at the photograph or plant to see where the leaves overlap and which way they tilt; quite small changes can make a lot of difference. When satisfied, either stick the paper shapes in place or draw round them on paper.

In this case, the leaf shapes are to be treated in a simple way by cutting them out of fabric and applying them with just a few stitches, so the background could be given more attention. If you look into trees or plants, the spaces between are often dark or shaded. Therefore, if the spaces between the leaves on the paper are shaded with neutral colours and at the same time a filling stitch such as Cretan, seeding or straight stitch is drawn in, a working design sheet begins to emerge.

50 *Applied leaves, some of them overlapping, creating different tones. Very simple stitches, such as Cretan and fly stitch, are used to hold them in place*

Silk organza is a suitable fabric to use for this piece of work as it is firm to handle and can be dyed if necessary. Arrange the leaves, overlapping them where the design calls for it, and stitch in place using one or two fly stitches. Finish

51 *The photograph shows the squareness of hydrangea flowers when they are just opening*

by stitching the background in the chosen stitch. Again, the balance of fabric and stitch should complement each other and not look overworked.

Continuing with the idea of overlapping colours, small pieces or squares overlapped can provide intense points of colour. These can be held down in a very simple way just with a French knot or a small back stitch, or by using fly stitch which lies conveniently along two sides of a square. Squares of organzas can be frayed a little to thin the colour at the edges, giving a tonal effect. Small, intense areas like this placed among quieter areas help to provide focal points to a piece of work.

52 *The drawing emphasizes the shapes of the florets, and suggests one way of interpreting them, using squares of transparent fabrics*

53 *Another example of applying small squares of silk or nylon organzas, using fly stitch on the edges and then more fly stitches a little further away*

54 *Detail of Fig. 53*

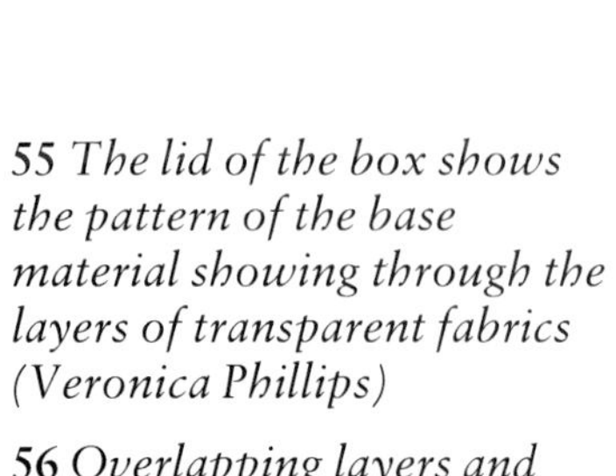

55 *The lid of the box shows the pattern of the base material showing through the layers of transparent fabrics (Veronica Phillips)*

56 *Overlapping layers and shapes, some of them gathered, are held in place by different densities of stitching (Ros Chilcott)*

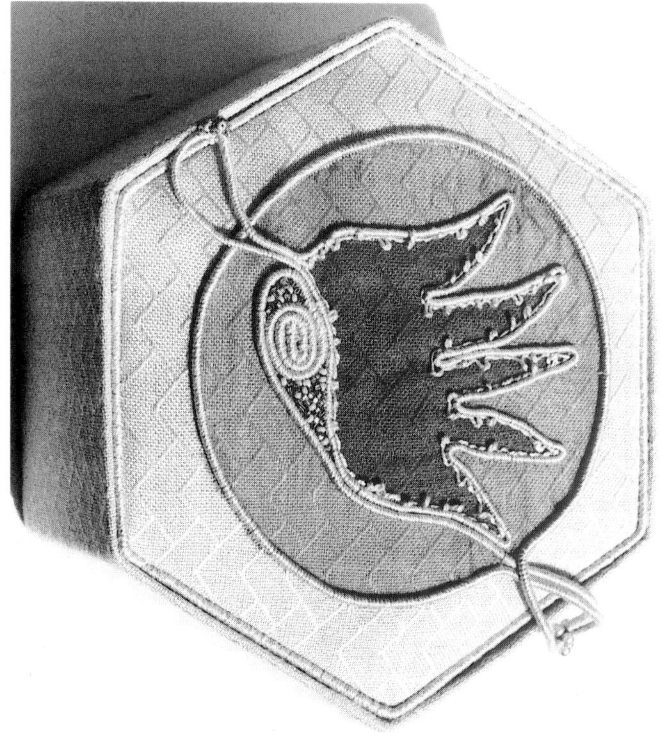

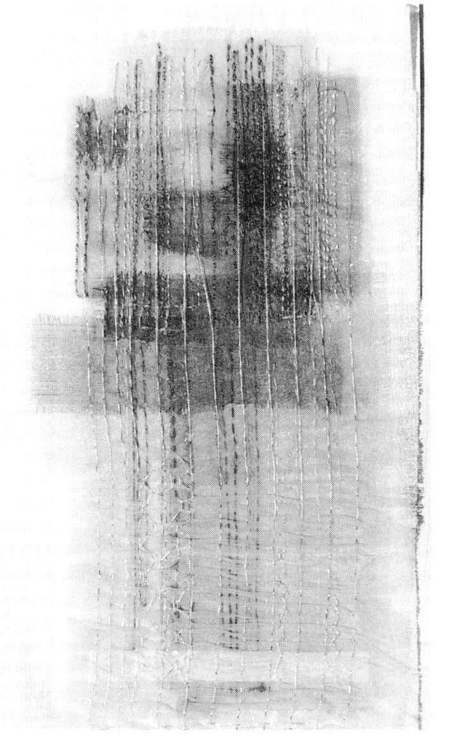

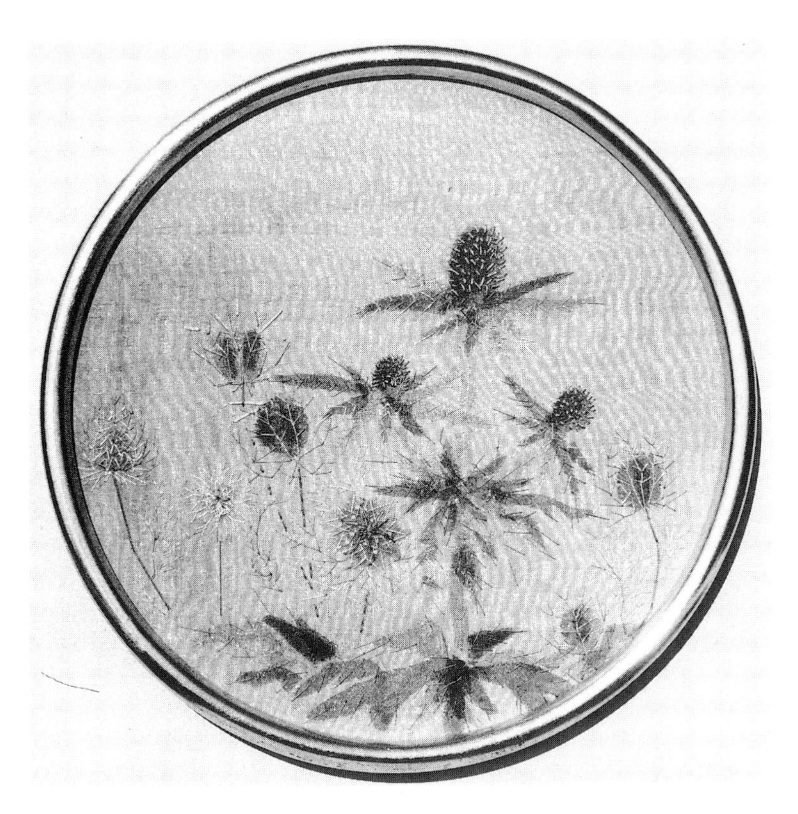

57 *Overlapping transparent fabrics and free stitching, used to freely interpret a plant idea (Mariel Stapledon)*

58 *Horses, worked in organdie and surface stitchery (Herta Puls)*

Reverse appliqué

There seems to be some confusion about the term 'reverse appliqué'. The following method should not be used to describe the method of appliqué used by the Cuna Indians of the San Blas Islands to make their molas.

59 *Reverse appliqué was used for this interpretation of winter trees. The embroidery was started with three layers of very fine transparent gauzes, hardly yellow, hardly blue and white. Different areas were cut away to give the impression of winter skies and water, before adding surface stitchery*

Instead of adding layers one to another, this method starts with all the layers together. After stitching through all the layers, one area after another is cut away to reveal the fabric underneath. Using transparent fabrics means that not only can the layers be cut away from the top, but from underneath as well. As one fabric over another creates a different tone, many subtle effects can be achieved.

Select a few squares of different-coloured transparent fabrics the size of the finished piece, with the grain of the materials matching. These can be a mixture of plain or patterned organzas, synthetic or silk; layers of net can also be included. Stitch the design through all the layers, using back stitch and making quite sure that the shapes are enclosed.

Using a small, sharp pair of scissors and starting in the middle of the selected shape to be cut away, very carefully make a snip in the fabric. Checking that only one layer is being cut, move towards the stitched edge of the shape. Cut along the edge of the stitching, taking care not to cut any of the stitches. After the first layer has been cut away, it may be decided that two layers need removing, in which case the process can be repeated. It is more satisfactory to remove one layer at a time. If the top layer, or the top two layers are to be left, cut away the bottom layers to the required level.

The edges now need to be neatened and strengthened. This can be done by stitching over them, using herringbone stitch or buttonhole stitch, or by couching a suitable thread along the edge. Further decorative stitching may be added if the design requires it. This technique can also be worked on the machine (see Chapter 4).

There is no precise number of layers for this technique. Indeed, I once had a student use twelve, but equally very good designs can be made by using only two or three layers. Unexpected effects can result from placing coloured paper or fabric behind the finished piece of work.

Reverse appliqué is best used where an element of surprise can be accepted, as it is difficult to plan with accuracy the effect of cutting away the layers. For this reason, however, it is fun to do and can be rewarding.

Bonded appliqué

A method of appliqué which should not be ignored is that of using iron-on adhesive. This is available as a web, either on non-stick paper or already coated onto Vilene. Either way, the transparent fabric will be stiffened, the Vilene giving a thickness with the added layer. This can be varied according to the weight of the Vilene used, and some are extremely lightweight.

If you are using the paper-backed web, this is ironed onto the transparent fabric, after which the paper is peeled away. This fabric can then be applied by ironing it to wherever it is needed. In all cases, the web will prevent the fabric from fraying.

A more creative use could be to start with a piece of iron-on Vilene or web applied to a chosen fabric, and then to add a mixture of fine materials such as silk or cotton muslins, organdies or organzas, and nets. Amongst these could also be added threads of different thickness. The whole area should be then covered with non-stick paper to protect the iron, and then ironed all over to apply the fabrics to the background. Because the fabrics are thin, the adhesive will bond more than one layer; this will give an uneven surface as there will not be a uniform adhesion, but interesting surfaces and atmospheres can be created. The resulting fabric could be machined into or hand stitched, though it must be said that hand stitching through the adhesive is not as easy as without it.

Appliqué on net

Carrickmacross lace was an Irish lace of the nineteenth century. Technically it was not a lace at all, but consisted of motifs of muslin or mull which were applied onto net. Transparent fabrics are very suitable for this type of appliqué as net is a good support and quite strong, but needs the delicate quality to be maintained. Its main use is in the making of wedding veils. As this technique is particularly suitable to be worked on the machine, it will be dealt with in more depth in Chapter 4.

CHAPTER **4**

Machine embroidery

Although the sewing machine has been in common usage for over a hundred years, and has always been associated with embroidery, it is only very recently that it has come to be accepted as just another tool as a means to an end. It would be a mistake to think of it as a substitute for hand embroidery, as the results are quite different. However, many techniques worked by hand can be considered for the machine, including some of the ones already described. In addition, some effects can only be made with a machine, particularly those using dissolvable fabric.

It might be thought that delicate, transparent fabrics would be unsuitable for the machine, but this is not at all the case, although special care is sometimes needed.

Choosing a machine

Whether you are using transparent fabrics or other types of material, an understanding of what the machine can do is necessary before you can fully enjoy using it.

Most domestic sewing machines on sale today are capable of stitching a straight line, with an adjustment for altering the length of the stitch. In addition, they will usually work a zigzag stitch. The embroiderer will also need a machine able to do darning, as the adjustments for darning are the same as those required for working free embroidery. Another useful item to check when buying a machine is that it will take a twin needle. Automatic embroidery stitches can be useful, but they are not at all essential for machine embroidery in the creative sense.

A free arm is needed by the dressmaker, but the embroiderer needs a good-sized 'bed', on which the frame rests when working free embroidery. The ease with which adjustments can be made should also be taken into consideration when buying a machine; it is advisable to try one or two before making a purchase. It might also be useful to check the following:

1 Can the feed dog (or teeth) be lowered easily? This is usually done by pressing a button. If, instead of dropping the feed, a plate is needed to cover the teeth, the distance between the end of the needle and the bed on which the frame rests is reduced. This causes the needle to catch on the frame, thus damaging the needle and causing irritation.
2 Check how easily the various pressure feet can be changed. Again, check whether the distance left after removing the foot allows an embroidery frame to be put in place easily.
3 Can the zigzag lever be moved from straight stitch to full zigzag width easily, or does it have to be put into pre-set widths?
4 Is there a good support for a frame to rest upon?

When buying a new machine, it is worth finding out if a course of instruction is available, as this can save a lot of time and prove invaluable.

Each make of machine has its own range of attachments which have been engineered for precise reasons. It is only

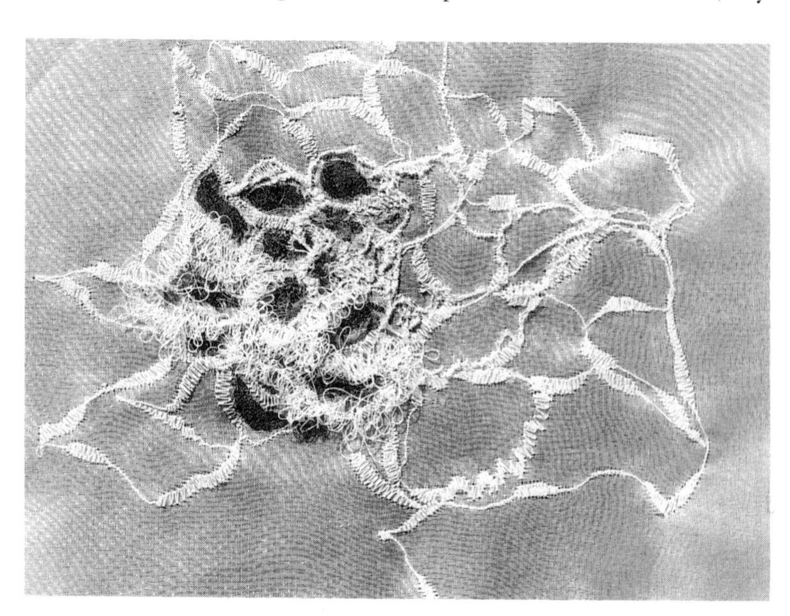

60 *The tacking foot has been used to produce a frothy effect*

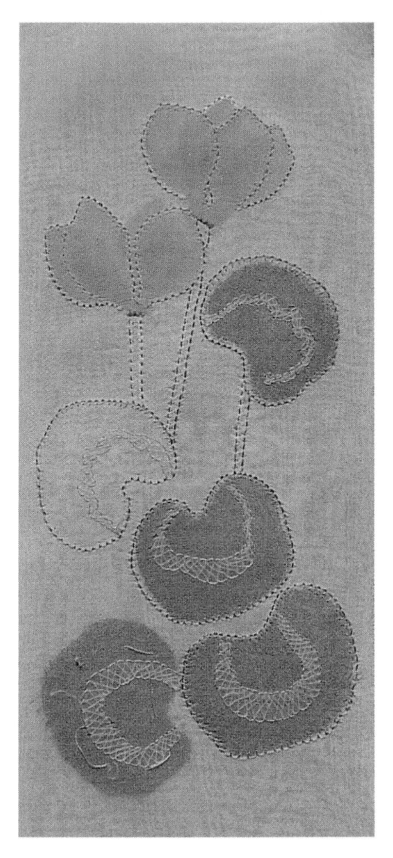

1 *Cyclamen flowers, using shadow appliqué*

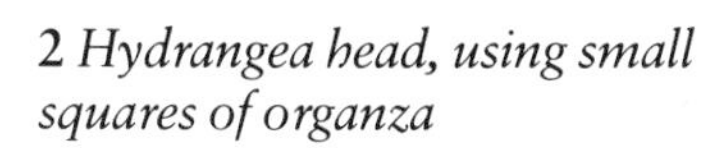

2 *Hydrangea head, using small squares of organza*

3 *Overlapping transparent fabrics on a dark background, with stitchery using gold threads, create a rich textile (Brenda Miller)*

4 Woven strips of dyed muslin

5 A landscape using shadow work and shadow quilting

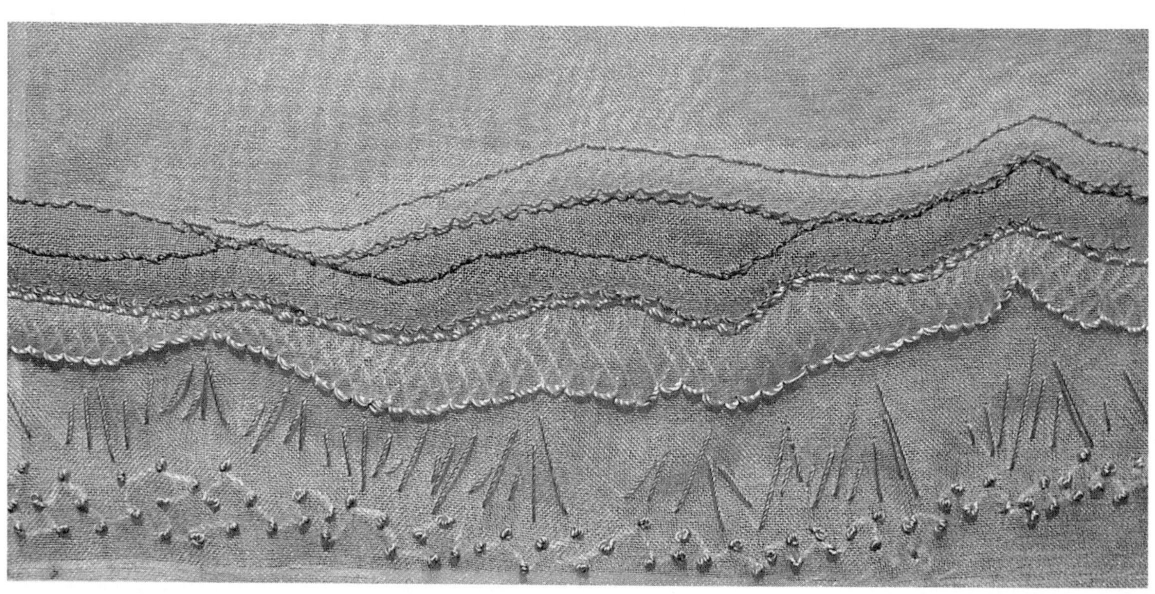

6 A hanging based on geometric shapes (Amanda Clayton)

7 Embroidery evolved from the colours of bulbs

9 A detail of the wedding dress

10 The two embroidered layers of the wedding dress sleeve

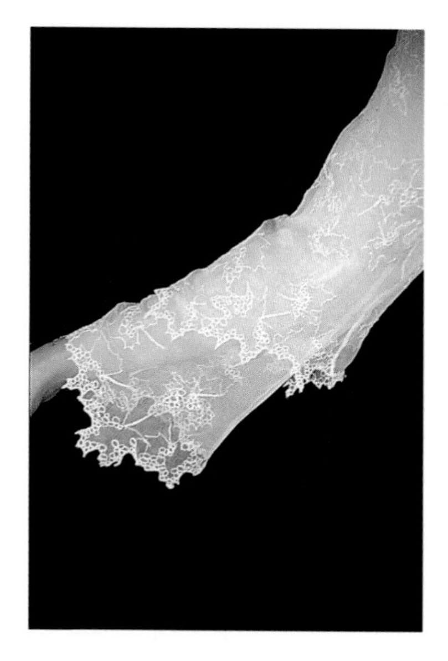

8 A hanging using transparent fabrics and Log Cabin patchwork (Jenny Bullen)

11 *'View across the Channel'. The graduated sky was achieved by overlaying different colours of nylon crystal organza*

12 *'Autumn Mists'. Two layers were used. The bottom layer of silk organza was embroidered using frayed strips for the trees. The top layer was embroidered on silk organza which was stippled with fabric dye under the stitching*

13 *'Viewpoint'. The wire netting was embroidered on silk organza, and laid over a background of dyed and machined habotai silk*

14 *Delphiniums, using dyed silk muslin*

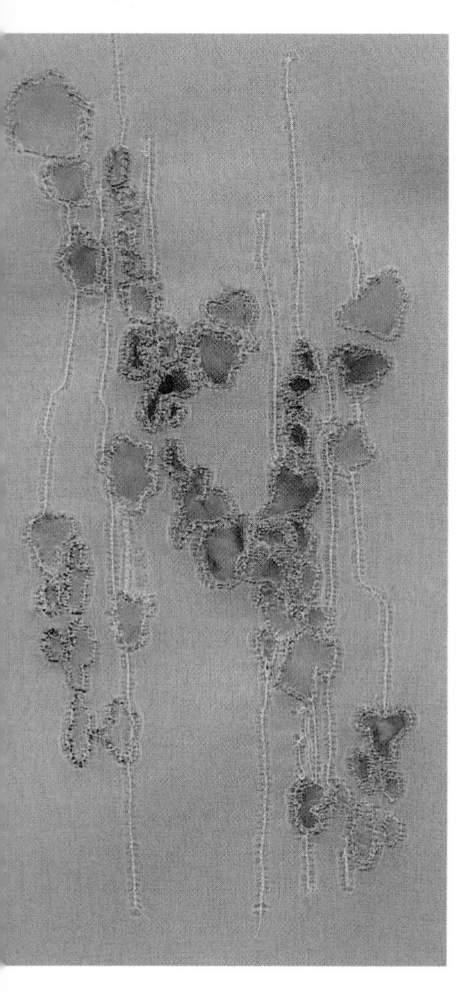

15 *An interpretation of the pattern found on a crumbling brick (see Fig. 71)*

16 *Winter trees, using three layers of pale colours with areas cut away*

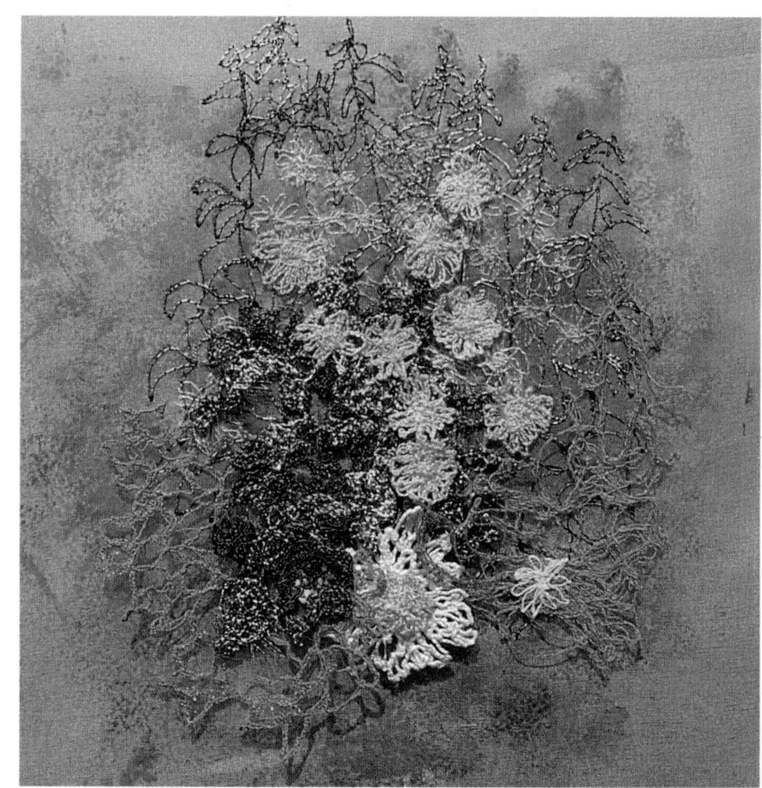

17 *Machine embroidery on a dyed organza background, with small individual motifs made on cold water-soluble material*

common sense to spend a little time getting to know which foot is required for different operations. If you look underneath the feet, you can see that they have different groove patterns and these determine how the machine will stitch. The embroidery foot is usually shorter than the others, enabling ease of movement.

Needles

It should be noted that different machines have different needle systems; it is important to use the correct one to give trouble-free stitching.

When inserting a needle, be sure to follow the manufacturer's instructions. As a rule, the side of the needle with the groove in it should be facing you. If you remember that the thread must lie in this groove in order to make the stitch, it can be a guide to the size of needle required. Some of the newer, exciting threads tend to shred and break; it is worth trying a larger-size needle to see if the thread lies more easily in the needle groove.

The correct choice of needle is important whatever the fabric being used. The range extends from the very fine number 60 up to 120, for use on really heavy fabric such as tough denim.

Apart from the variation in needle size, there is a variation in type of needle:

1 *Teflon-coated needles* slide through fabric easily and reduce static. They are suitable for use on stretch fabrics and also on fine ones.
2 *Ballpoint needles* part the threads when stitching in the same way that a tapestry needle does when stitching by hand, and so do not split the threads or cause puckering.
3 *Leather needles* need to be used with caution as they can cut the fabric.
4 *Twin needles* are useful to the dressmaker as well as the embroiderer, for they can make decorative effects with the ease of straight stitching. They consist of two needles joined together at the top into one shank, which fits into the machine like any other needle.

   Twin needles stitch in parallel lines, the distance between the lines being governed by the distance between the needles. Although the stitched lines are parallel on the surface, the threads cross underneath. The needles can be bought with a 2 mm, 3 mm and 4 mm space. Caution should be exercised when using these needles with a zigzag; a narrow zigzag can be used with the 2 mm size, but if used with the 4 mm there is the danger that the needles might hit the throat plate and break. If a short stitch is used, a more corded effect is obtained; with a longer stitch, the result is flatter. On transparent fabrics the crossing of the threads on the wrong side shows as a shadow, making an attractive pattern similar to shadow work.

As two needles need threading, obviously two reels of thread are required, but this problem can be easily overcome by winding a bobbin spool to act as the second reel. Follow the manufacturer's instructions for threading the needles.

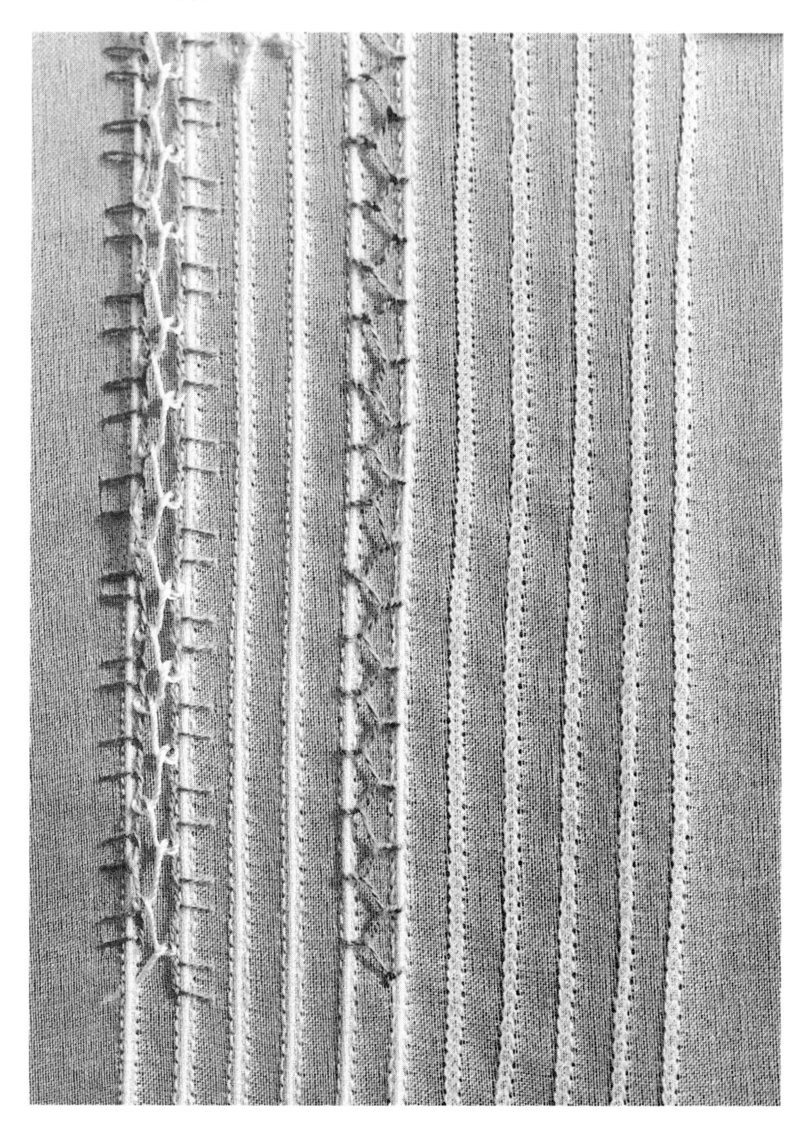

61 *When using a twin needle with transparent fabrics, the back of the stitch can be seen. If a thicker thread is wound onto the bobbin, this shows and also produces a corded line. The sample shows how insertion stitches can be combined with the raised lines*

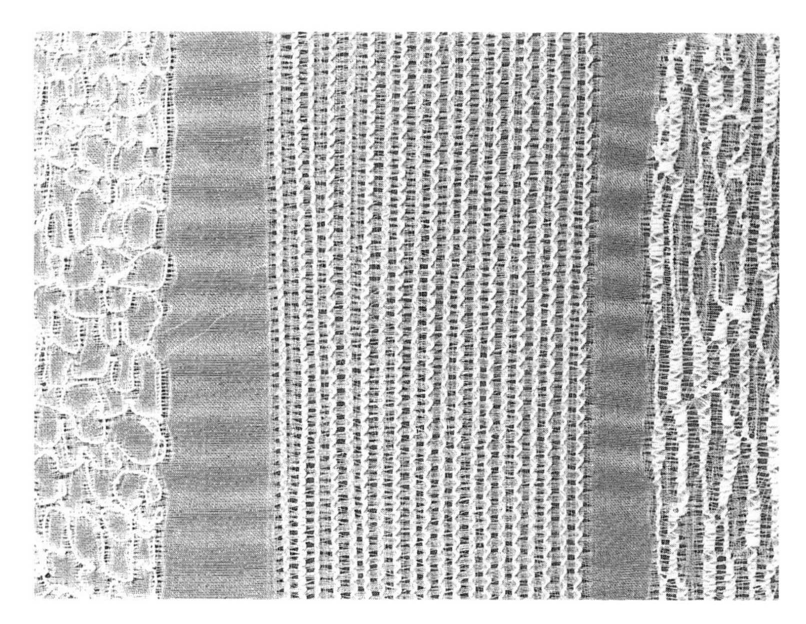

62 *This shows the difference between when the hem stitch needle is used with the foot for straight stitching, and when it is used for free machining. The free machining shows the result of using a straight stitch and a zigzag setting*

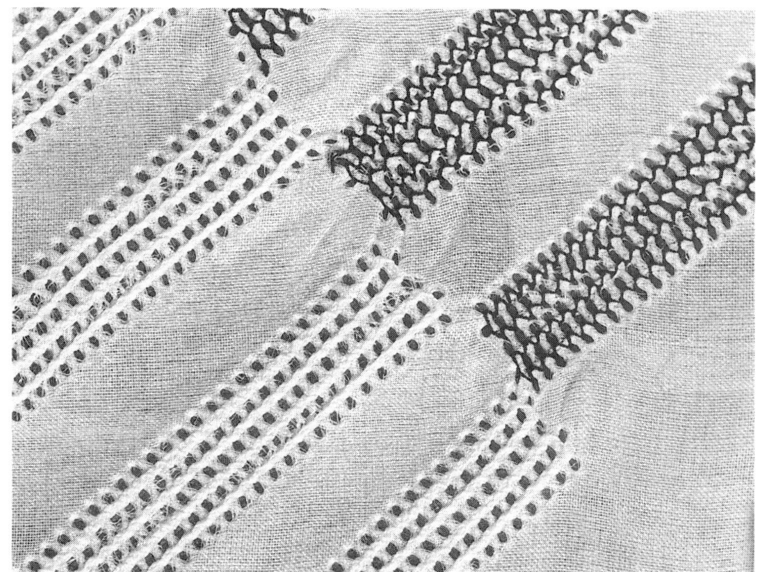

63 *The hem stitch needle used with double material and stitched across the bias. A contrasting thread produces a different effect*

5 *Hem stitch needles* are available for certain machines and have what looks like a spear shape. They work on fine fabrics and produce a beautiful hem stitch effect. The double needle produces a straight stitch and a hem stitch at the side of it. Again, care should be taken if using the zigzag that the swing is no wider than the space allowed in the foot. These needles work particularly well on double material and on the bias. The single needle can be used for free embroidery, and often works best where the colour of thread matches the colour of the fabric.

64 *This interpretation of the hedgerow flower, Queen Anne's lace, shows the use of whip stitch. The bottom tension is very loose, therefore the bottom thread is pulled through to the surface. The transparent fabric, in this case organdie, was worked on both sides, to give a feeling of depth*

Tensions

The stitch made on the domestic sewing machine is called a lock stitch, and is made by a thread from the bottom twisting round a thread from the top. When the same thread is used for the top and the bottom, and the tensions on those threads are even, the twist is made in the fabric and a very even line of stitching is made, which is usually required by the dressmaker. If, for any reason, one of the threads is of a different thickness, this could alter the tension, and an adjustment might need to be made. With such a variety of threads on the market today, it makes sense for this reason alone to understand how to make adjustments to both the top and the bottom tensions in order to use the machine on a very basic level. Happily, these adjustments are the very same ones needed to use the machine in a more exciting and creative way.

If the tensions are even, the threads twist in the middle of the fabric so that little of the bottom thread is seen on the top, and little of the top thread is seen on the bottom. It is useful when testing tensions to have a different-coloured thread top and bottom in order to see clearly what is happening. If the bottom thread tension is loose, it will be pulled through to the top side and will be seen quite clearly wrapping around the top thread. Equally, if the top thread tension is looser than the bottom one, the top thread will be pulled through to the bottom side. To use the machine in a creative way, we often need to exploit these effects. For instance, by deliberately loosening the bottom tension, the bottom thread will be pulled through to the surface and whip around the top thread, hence its name – whip stitch. With the foot in place and an average-length stitch, this can look unattractive, but if a very short stitch is used a corded line can be the result.

A thick thread such as coton perlé no. 5 or thick embroidery cotton, which would be too thick to thread through the needle, can be wound onto a bobbin and used as the lower thread. In this case, the bottom thread is the important one and therefore the underside of the fabric will be the right side. Being a thick thread in the bobbin, this thread will not pull through the fabric but will lie on the underside and be couched down by the top thread. Obviously, having such a thick thread on the bottom means that the lower tension will need to be loosened, simply for it to pass through the tension spring.

The top tension is usually set by a dial, so this should be set to the normal number recommended for the machine. The lower numbers loosen the tension, and the higher ones tighten it. The pressure bar of the machine is usually raised when the machine is not in use, but it is just as well to check this when threading the top thread; when the pressure bar is lowered the tension discs close, and this would prevent the top thread getting between them, resulting in the top thread having no tension and causing jamming.

The lower thread tension is altered by regulating the tiny screw on the bobbin case. This statement often causes alarm, but need not do so if certain precautions are taken. Before altering anything, and while the machine is threaded for even-tension sewing, remove the bobbin and its case from the machine and gently pull the thread to get the feel of it. It is advisable to spend a little time on this, as recognizing this feel will make it easy to return the tension to normal after any alterations have been made. There should be just a suggestion of resistance. Some machines are not fitted with removable bobbin cases; if this is the case, simply pull the thread as it lies in the machine.

Whatever the thickness of the thread being used, if normal tension is required, adjust the screw until the thread gives the feel of slight resistance.

A word of warning. The screw has a very short shank, so when any alteration is being made, do it over a piece of felt or a box lid so that if the screw does fall out it will not be lost. The alternative is to buy another bobbin case for embroidery use.

Exercises to try with the foot on the machine

1 Start with a normal-length straight stitch and gradually increase the zigzag from 0 to full width.
2 Repeat this from the smallest-length stitch up to the longest one.
3 Loosen the bottom tension and repeat exercises 1 and 2.
4 Wind a thick thread in the bobbin and, using a medium-length stitch, make a few parallel lines of couching. Remember that the *wrong* side of the fabric will be uppermost and the couched lines will be underneath.

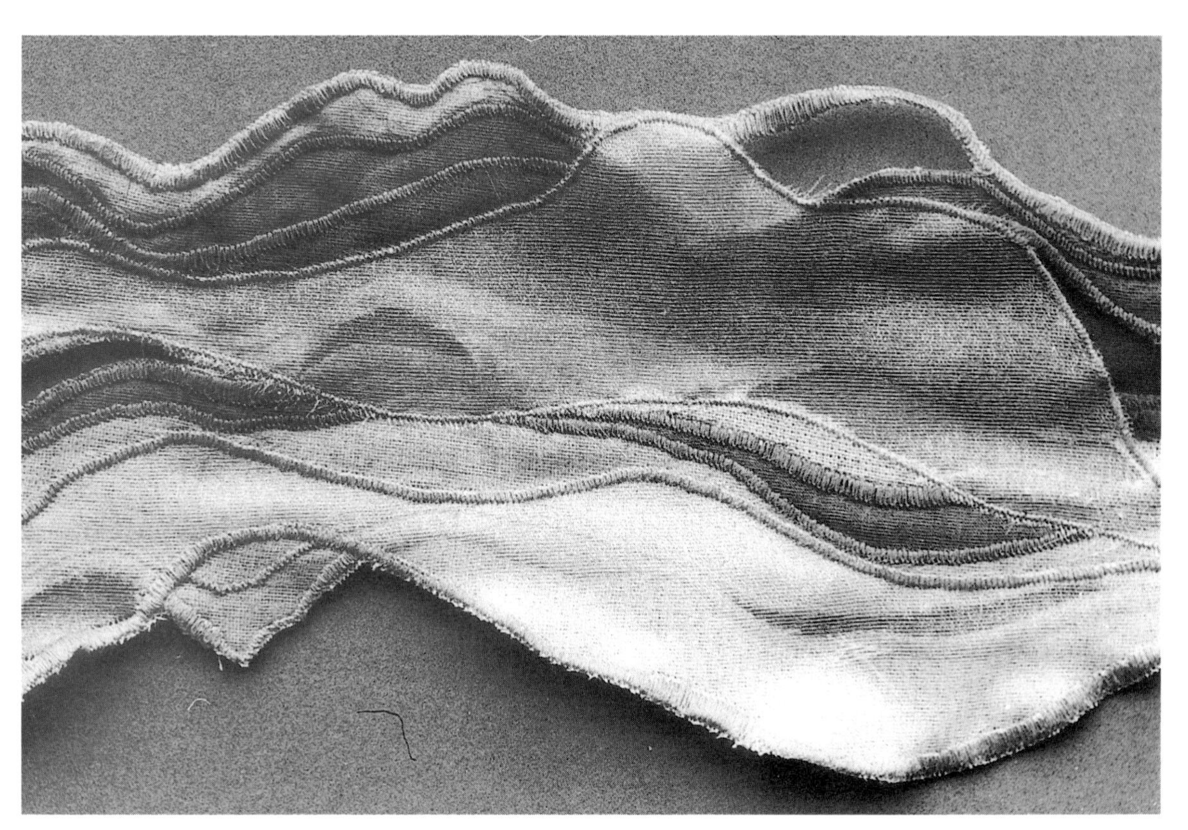

65 *Different rhythms of lines and layers of transparent fabrics edged with different widths of zigzag stitch (Julia Sylvester)*

Free machine embroidery

Whereas machining in the normal way produces straight lines with a uniform length of stitch, by making two simple adjustment to the machine it is possible to use it in a completely different way:

1 Remove the pressure foot.
2 Lower the feed dog (or teeth).

In fact, follow the maker's instructions for darning.

The fabric for free machining must be stretched in a round embroidery frame until it is very taut. This is done by alternately stretching the fabric across the straight of the grain and tightening the screw on the hoop. The pleasure and the success of free machine embroidery depends upon this preparation, so it is worth the effort to get it right. When this has been done, using your thumbs, gently press the inside ring so that the fabric is just proud of the outside ring; this will ensure that the fabric sits on the bed of the machine when stitching.

Some very fine fabrics, such as silk muslin used for the wedding dress described in Chapter 8, need extra precautions when tightening in the embroidery frame, otherwise the material splits. This problem can be overcome by cutting two pieces of cotton material large enough to fit in the frame. From each piece, cut out a circle 5 cm (2 in) *smaller* than the diameter of the frame and discard, retaining the two rings of fabric. Bind the inner circle of the frame with tape, then sandwich the fabric to be embroidered between the two rings of cotton material. The fine silk can then be stretched as the cotton layers take the strain.

Slip the hoop under the needle. This is where the third vital adjustment must be made, to lower the pressure bar. This is all too easily forgotten when there is not a foot, but until the pressure bar is lowered there is no tension on the top thread; consequently the very loose top thread will be pulled through to the other side and will become wrapped around the race and jam the machine.

Having checked that the pressure foot is down, bring the bottom thread through to the surface. Hold the top and the bottom threads while two or three stitches are made, and then they can be cut off. It is important to do this, otherwise the threads become caught up in the stitching and in the case of fine fabrics would show through and look unsightly.

66 *'Scribbling' with the free machine setting*

Holding the edges of the hoop, move it around as smoothly as possible. The two controls now in use are the speed of moving the hoop, which determines the length of the stitch made, and the speed at which the machine is run. The other control which it is possible to use is the zigzag. After a little practice at 'scribbling', the tension alterations might be tried.

Techniques using the machine

Appliqué

The techniques so far described for hand stitching on transparent fabrics can also be used on the machine. Appliqué is one such technique. When applying one shape to another, the weight of the fabrics should be considered:

whereas a fine material might be applied to a heavier-weight background, it would be inadvisable to apply a thick fabric to a very fine one as this might stretch and distort it.

Cutting a shape from a fine fabric to apply to another fabric can cause problems using the machine; the fabric could become floppy and difficult to work with, and would probably stretch in the handling. A more satisfactory method is to cut a piece of material and mark on it the shape to be applied. Tack this in position, with the warp and weft matching those of the background fabric. Machine round the shape and cut away the excess. Machine round the edge a second time, using a suitable width zigzag and a short-length stitch to make a satin stitch edge.

When using this method, the design can either be marked out with a watercolour pencil or with a water-soluble marker, or, and this applies particularly if the shape is to be repeated, a template could be cut, pinned in position and stitched round.

Variations

Depending on the purpose of the article being appliquéd, whether it is purely decorative or is to take some wear, different treatments of the edges of the applied piece could be considered:

1 Instead of satin stitch round the shape, work two or three lines of straight stitch.
2 If you use a twin needle, this makes a more pronounced edge.
3 Using free machining, many different edges could be made. Some parts could be crisp and sharp, while others might be made more diffuse by overstitching the edge onto the background.

As well as applying a precise shape, small pieces of organzas can be incorporated when machining, contrasting the different areas of smooth colour and the different textures of stitch.

Another form of appliqué is the one used in the illustration of delphiniums (Fig. 68). Strips of silk muslin were dyed and gathered, then placed in position on the background and the characteristic shapes of the individual flowers machined.

The background to the delphinium panel has another form of appliqué, if that really is the correct term for it. A number of scraps of fabrics were held in position by placing

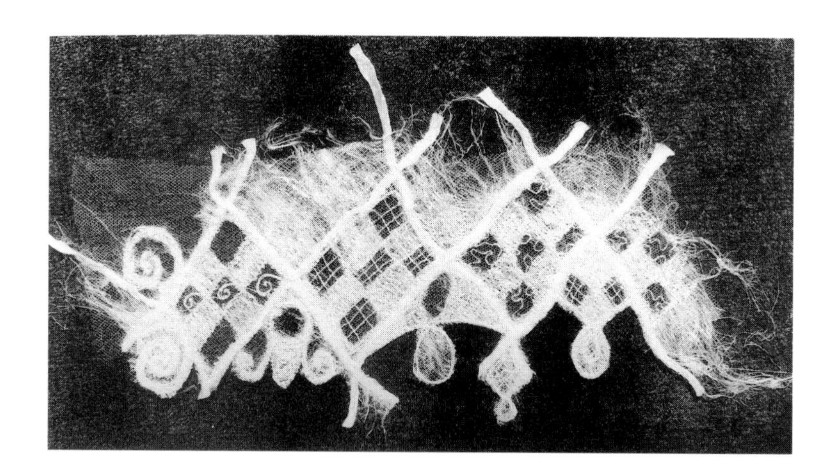

67 *Fine rouleaux and handmade felt, cut and applied to a net background (Amanda Clayton)*

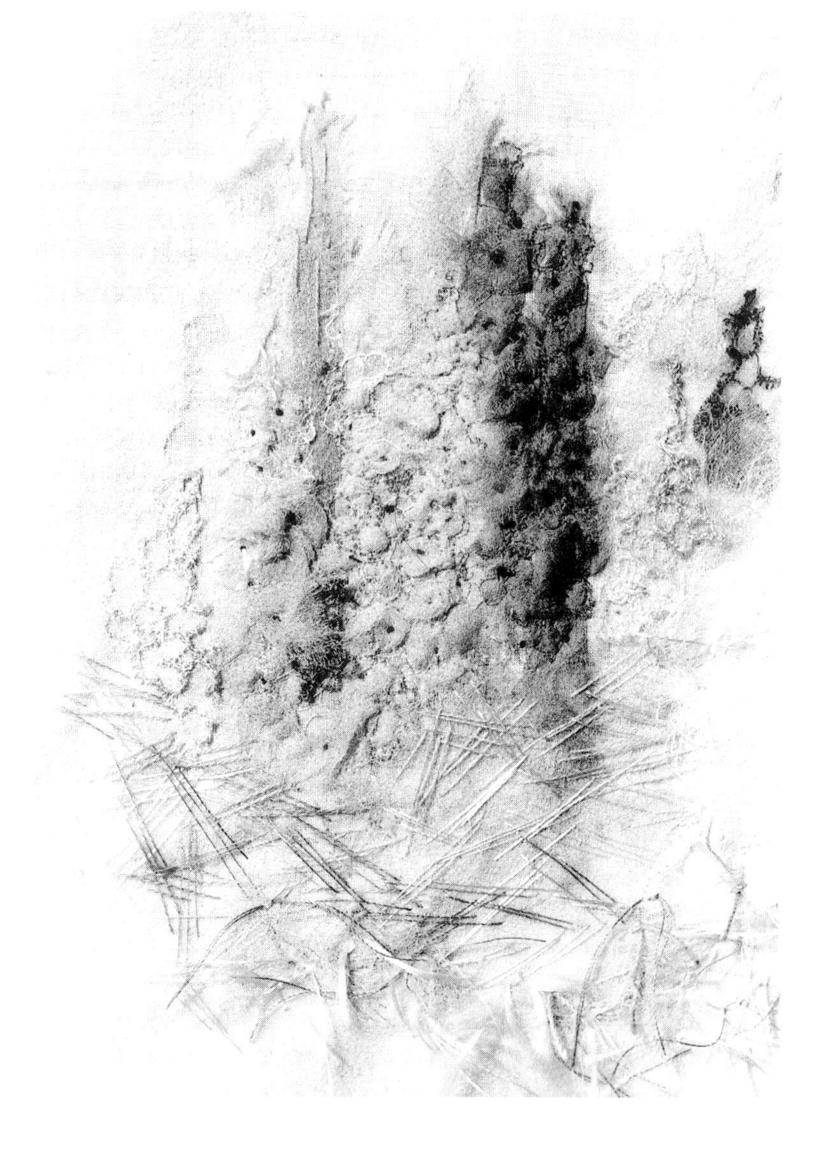

68 *Delphiniums interpreted from strips of dyed silk muslin, plus fragments worked on cold-water-soluble material, with some hand stitching*

amongst them small pieces of iron-on web. The panel was finished with some hand stitching of straight stitches and single tufted knots. The idea was to show the mixture of layers and textures found in any growing area.

Shadow appliqué

Using the machine for this technique needs the same preparation as when working by hand (see p. 49–50). However, instead of using pin stitch to fix all the layers together, the shapes sandwiched between the bottom and the top layers can be held in place by stitching with the machine, using a single or a twin needle. The stitching could be made with the foot on the machine, or by free machining. In either case, it might be found easier to work with the fabric mounted in an embroidery hoop.

Variations

Using a hem stitch needle with the foot on the machine gives a similar appearance to pin stitch worked by hand. Alternatively, the hem stitch needle could be used with free machining.

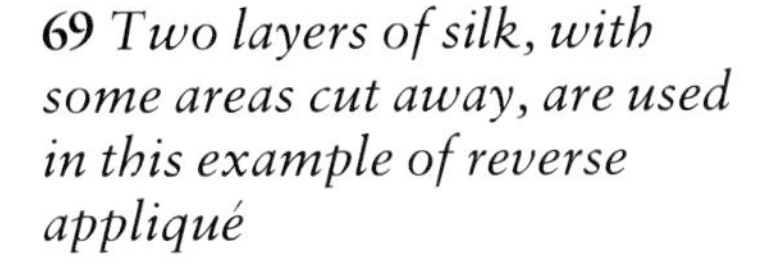

69 *Two layers of silk, with some areas cut away, are used in this example of reverse appliqué*

Reverse appliqué

The machine is an ideal tool to use for reverse appliqué. As explained in Chapter 3, if all the layers used are transparent, any layer may be revealed by cutting away layers, either from the top downwards or from the bottom upwards. Apart from the colour of the layer being revealed, the colour beneath will affect the tone, sometimes with surprising results.

The benefit of using the machine for reverse appliqué is that, by setting the machine for free embroidery, the stitching round the shapes can be done quite quickly. By using a small stitch, a strong line of stitching is made through all the layers of material. Another advantage of the method is that small or intricate shapes can be made, which would be more difficult to achieve by applying a separate

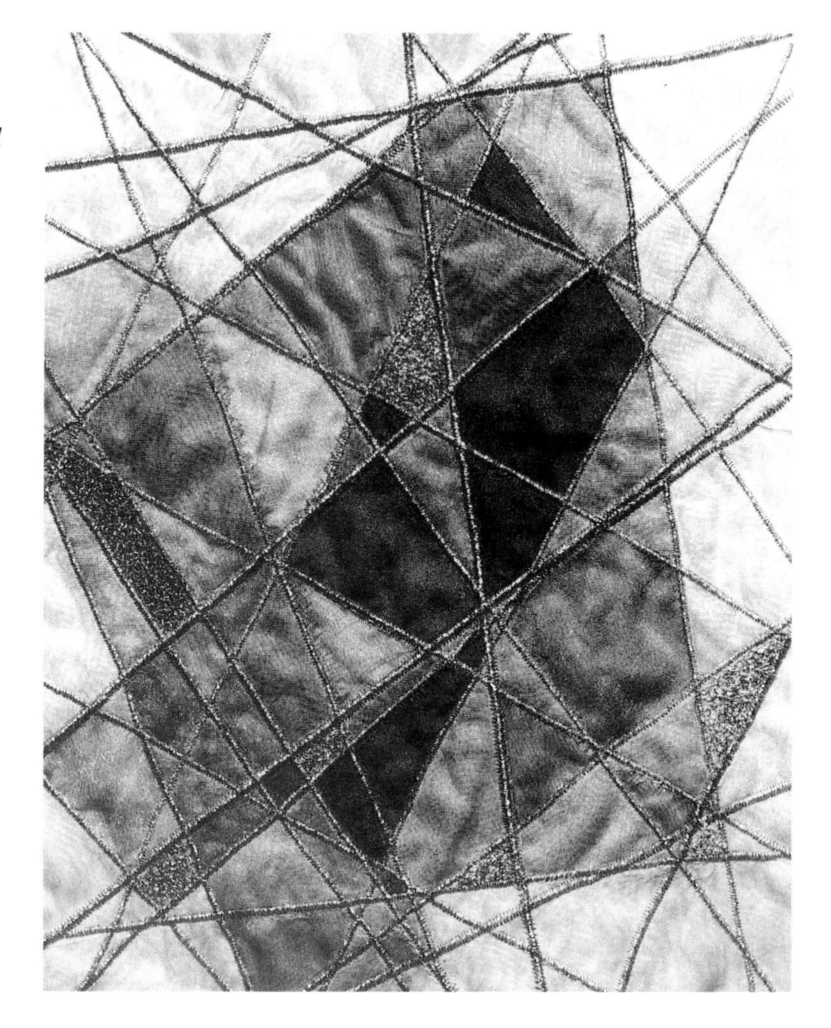

70 *Reverse appliqué, using many layers of transparent fabrics. The grid lines are stitched with a metallic thread (Doreen Plews)*

piece of material. After the various layers have been cut away, the raw edges can be neatened, either by use of the zigzag or by decorative 'scribbling' over the edges. Any further embroidery can then be added.

Inlay

A form of inlay can be worked on the machine. To define the the term, this means cutting out a shape from a fabric and inserting in the hole another material of the same shape, so that the finished work is one layer of fabric. Fig. 71 shows an inlay embroidery based on the pattern found on an old brick:

1 The design was traced on a piece of organza.
2 The organza was placed over a piece of space-dyed silk and tacked in place.
3 The organza was stretched in an embroidery hoop.
4 The shapes were machined, using free machining and a hem stitch needle.
5 The organza shapes were cut away to reveal the dyed fabric underneath.
6 The fabric was turned over, and the excess dyed material was cut away to the stitching line.

71 *The shaded area shows the pattern found on a crumbling old brick. The reverse repeat shows how the design might be extended. This design could be worked on a large or a small scale, and could be interpreted in a variety of techniques*

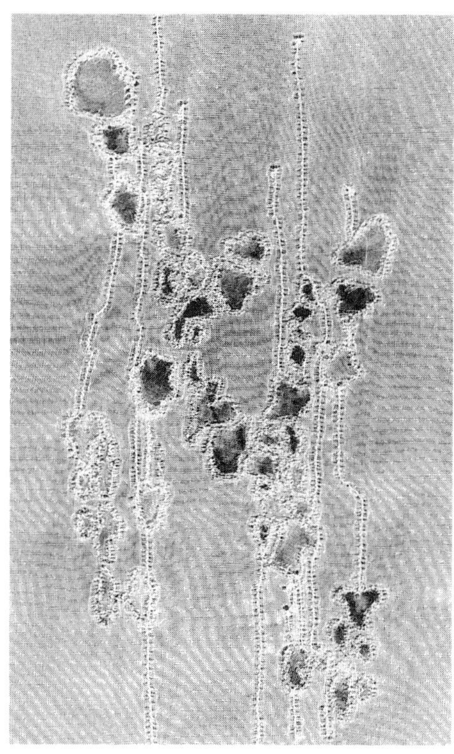

72 *One interpretation of the brick design*

73 *The corner of the net has been embroidered, using cold-water-soluble material. The appliqué shows the motif of organza machined in place, with some organza still to be cut away*

Appliqué on net

Organzas, whether the beautifully coloured ones available or hand-painted or plain silk organza, can be applied to nets of all kinds in the manner of Carrickmacross lace (see p. 62). The technique is the same as for applying to other fabrics and could be used for making a really special bridal veil, or as a curtain to give particular interest to a room.

Variations

Instead of using plain fabric, the material to be used for the applied piece could be textured by machining over it with a whip stitch. Alternatively, where possible, the hem stitch needle could be used to make a lacy effect. (Generally speaking, this is better if a double piece of organza is used.)

Quilting

Most of the shadow quilting techniques can be carried out on the machine. Extra care is needed when working Italian quilting, otherwise the parallel lines are stitched over, making it impossible to thread through the quilting wool.

It is easier to stitch through felt using the machine than by hand, and this can provide a different way of approaching shadow quilting. Instead of stitching round the edges of the felt padding, lines of machining can cross the shapes, thus holding the shapes in place and giving a different look to the quilting. These lines might also be parallel and padded with wool, thus incorporating Italian quilting with shadow quilting.

Pulled fabric

Another technique which can be done on the machine is pulled work. This is no way duplicates hand pulled work, which relies on precision, but rather the lacy elements of pulled fabric. Not all fine fabrics pull well, but most do, particularly those with a loose weave such as fine muslins and voiles.

Both top and bottom tensions need to be slightly tightened. A strong thread such as cotton or one made from polyester is easier to work with, though other threads are worth trying; the metallic threads made for the machine can be very effective.

This method of pulling uses the zigzag to pull groups of threads together and is most obvious when the widest setting is used, though variations can be made by using a narrower setting. The fabric needs to be framed in a hoop as the threads are being pulled, as this provides resistance. For straight lines, the machining can be done with the foot in place, but many other interpretations can be made using free machining. The frame should be moved slowly, and the machine run fairly fast.

Fabric threads are pulled together along the warp and weft. Open grids can be made by first pulling the warp threads, and then turning the fabric 90% and pulling the weft threads.

When a shape is to be made, for instance a leaf shape, the outline should be worked first of all, and then the threads

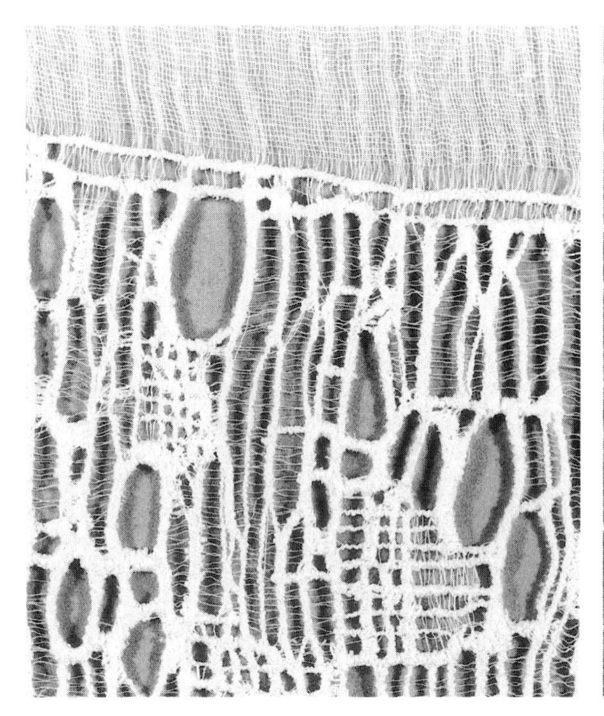

74 *Pulled fabric, using the machine to show the lacy effects which can be made with fine materials (Peggy Cronin)*

75 *A grid made by using a twin needle. The shapes are filled by using different needles and stitching across the spaces (Doreen Plews)*

inside the shape can be worked to make the inner pattern. Some of the lines made can be worked over a number of times to give emphasis, finally reworking the edge.

Although the fabric is snatched across the straight lines of the warp and the weft threads, travelling across diagonally can cause patterns to form behind the stitch.

Suitable subjects for lacy effects are butterflies, skeletal leaves, dragonflies or ripples on water.

Variations

1 The shapes embroidered in this way are firm enough to be cut out and used as appliquéd pieces, or as free-standing shapes.
2 After the shape has been worked but before the outline is finally worked, place a strip of really soft material, such as silk muslin, underneath, then remachine the outline. The soft material is pulled into the zigzag, backing the openwork easily, without having to cut out the shape or tack it in position.

Water-soluble fabrics

These fabrics act as a support while lacy textures are worked upon them. When the embroidery is finished, the

76 *Separate motifs have been worked, using coton perlé nos. 8 and 5 on cold-water-soluble fabric*

fabric is dissolved away.

There are two types of water-soluble fabric on the market, each with advantages and disadvantages, and it is worth trying both kinds to find which one you prefer. They are both suitable only for machine embroidery; this is not a hand embroidery technique.

The difference between the two fabrics is that one is soluble in hot water, while the other dissolves in cold water. The hot water method needs very hot water, even to the point of simmering, while the cold water fabric dissolves away as soon as it touches cold water. This means that care needs to be taken that surfaces and hands are quite dry when handling this material, and to sneeze can be disastrous!

The two materials look quite different, which makes it easy to distinguish between them when you are ready to dissolve the fabric. The one requiring hot water is pale blue and quite firm to handle. It can be mounted in a round embroidery hoop in the usual way, though it is advisable to bind the inner ring. The cold water fabric has the appearance of clear plastic and is slightly stretchy, so that care

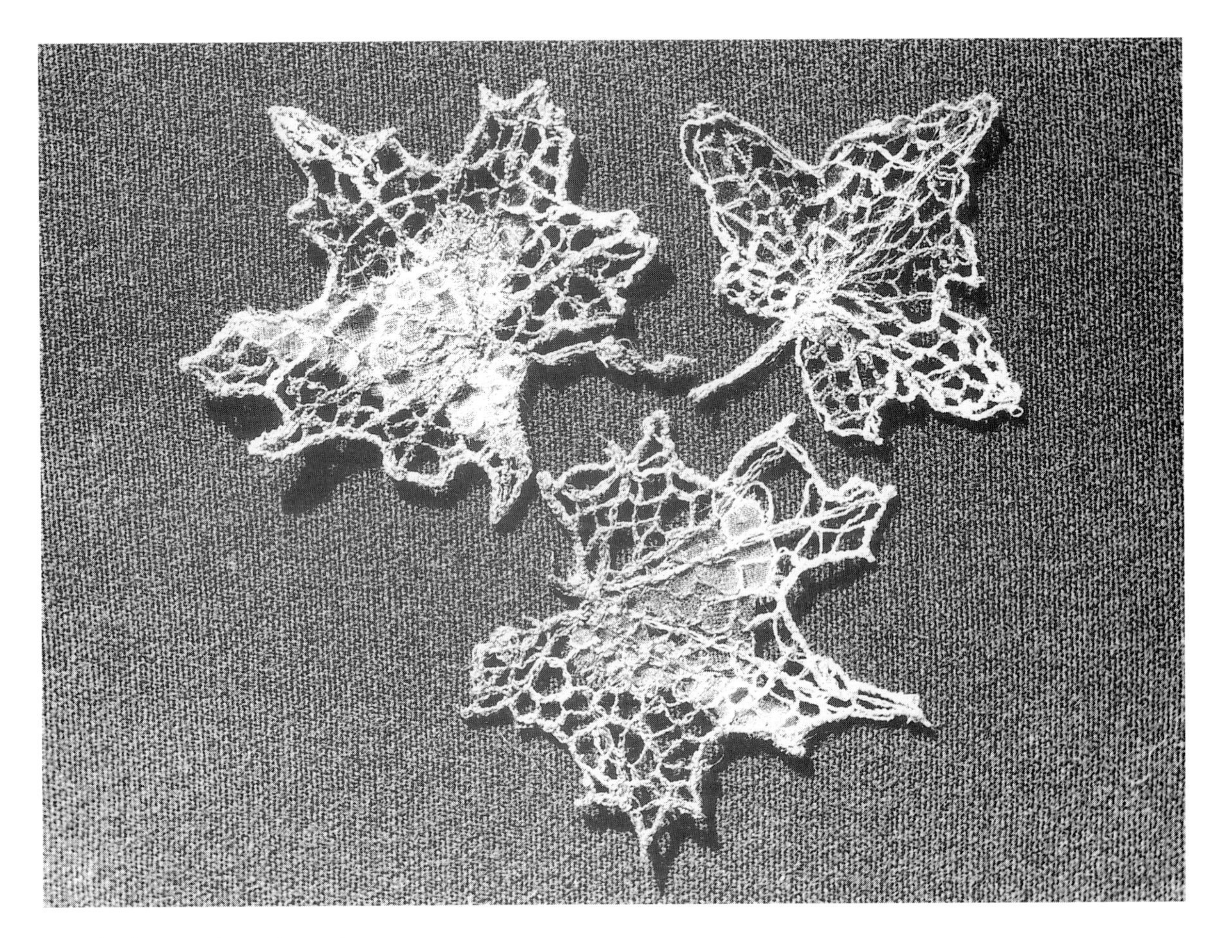

77 The leaves show how the machining needs to crisscross to hold together when using soluble fabric. In this sample, pieces of transparent fabric have been incorporated

78 Many separate leaves have been made and assembled to create foliage (Peggy Cronin)

is needed when mounting it in the frame. This material tears fairly easily and you may find it easier to work with a double layer in the frame.

It is possible to work with the usual threads on these materials, including shiny rayon threads and metallic ones, but to be on the safe side, particularly when very hot water is to be used, it is advisable to work a test piece first.

As the fabric will be dissolved when the stitching is finished, certain precautions should be taken. The most important is to crisscross the stitching, forming a web, so that when the fabric dissolves the web holds the threads together. Another important thing to remember is to use a

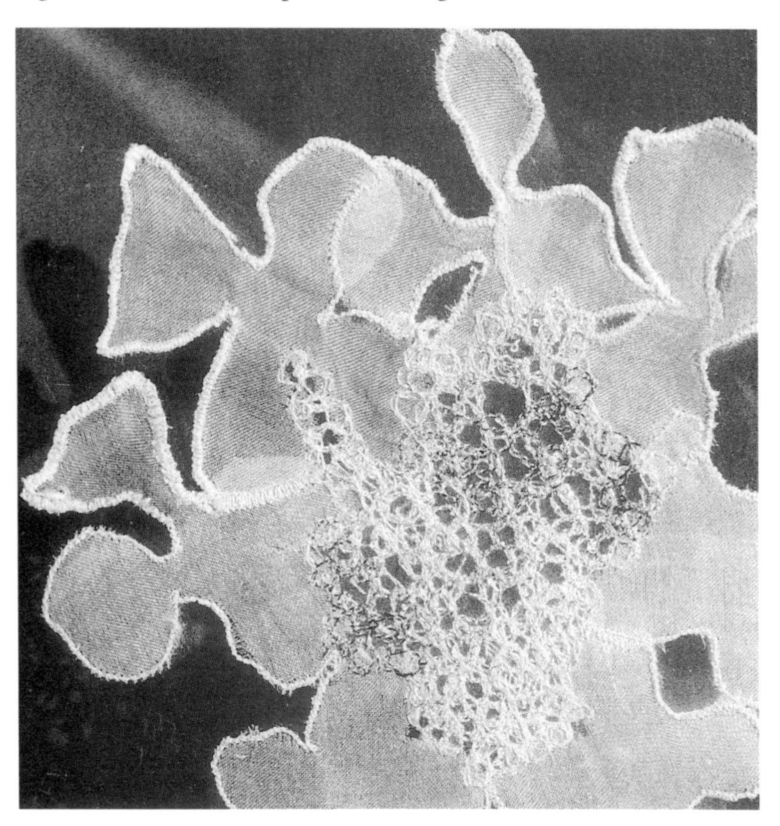

79 *In this interpretation of lace cap hydrangea, the outer organza florets were placed on cold-water-soluble fabric. The centre was machined in pinks and greens. The soluble material was a support to the outer florets when these were machined round the edge*

straight stitch setting on the machine to begin with, not a zigzag, as, without a fabric backing to hold the zigzag in place, it becomes just a very loose stitch. A zigzag can be used in the later stages.

Some thought should be given to marking out a design on these materials. If a water-soluble pencil is used, it could colour the threads when the work is immersed in water. Where suitable, cut out a template, place it on the fabric and machine round it, then remove the template and machine

80 *The edges of the silk muslin were machined over cold-water-soluble fabric, using a metallic thread with a figure-of-eight movement*

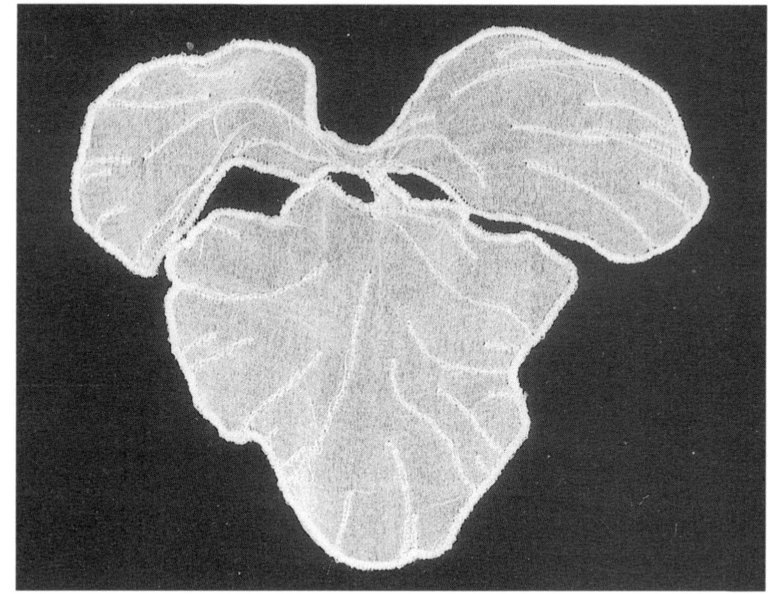

81 *A double layer of organza and silk muslin was machined in straight stitch and cut out. The shape was then mounted onto cold-water-soluble fabric, and the edges zigzag stitched over the original straight stitch*

82 *The lacy edge was worked over cold-water-soluble fabric, using a very fine polyester thread. To anchor it a little more firmly, a grid was machined over the web*

83 *A very controlled use of the machine and soluble fabric to interpret olive trees (Yanny Bennitt)*

over the shape. A suitable marker is one which can be wiped away with a damp cloth, as this dissolves away with the fabric.

Variations

1 Small pieces of coloured fabrics such as organzas or felts could be placed on and incorporated into the lacy stitching.
2 If a number of shapes are to be machined, make a lot of them, filling the frame before dissolving the background away.
3 A large area could be machined as a 'scribble', and then shapes cut out and used either free-standing or applied.
4 This material is a valuable aid when used as a support for satin stitching round the edge of a cut-out shape.

CHAPTER 5

Fabric paints and dyes

In recent years, fabric dyes and paints have become just as much an accepted tool of the embroiderer as the sewing machine or needle and thread, all methods to be used for interpreting an idea. In fact, colouring fabric to suit one's own purpose is not nearly as new an idea as might be thought. In the past, a piece of fabric was sometimes coloured to complete a piece of patchwork, and hands and faces were sometimes painted when figures featured in a piece of work. When dyeing or painting a piece of fabric, whether for a background or for use in patchwork, it is possible to keep control of the colour in the work and not be at the mercy of what is in the shops. Even when the right colour is available, often only small amounts of material are needed so that with an ample supply of materials in white, and a selection of paints and dyes, it is possible to be personal and individual in the use of colour. Home dyeing can never compete with the highly complex business of commercial dyeing but, used with discretion, it can be a great help to the embroiderer.

The danger lies in the over-use of paints and dyes. Especially when you start to use colour on fabric, there is a great temptation to paint in every detail, leaving no room for the embroidery except as an irrelevant extra. Painting a picture is one thing; using dyes to wash in a background, or to colour a piece of fabric or thread, is another. Used with sensitivity, fabric paints and dyes can be very effective in creating atmosphere and mood. From a practical point of view, they can be used to mark out a design on fabric, just as the final stage of the prick and pounce method uses a fine brush and colour to connect up the chalk dots which have been pounced through holes in tracing paper.

Fabric dyes and paints are sometimes thought to be an easy option, but they are not and, if not used with subtlety, will never enhance an embroidery. Having sounded warnings, they can be a delight to use, particularly on fine fabrics where one colour overlays another.

All fabrics should be well washed before dyeing.

Differences between fabric paints and fabric dyes

Paints and dyes are part of a highly technical industry, but a little understanding of their make-up can help in remembering and identifying their individual uses.

Fabric paints

Fabric paints are made from finely ground pigments held in suspension, usually in a thickened base. If watered down, these pigment particles will settle at the bottom as a sediment. Equally, if applied to fabric in a very dilute form, the colour particles will stay together and the water will bleed through the fabric, leaving a watermarked edge. These fabric paints are therefore usually used in their thickened state, though they can be diluted to a thin, creamy consistency. Fabric paints are sold in full-strength colours, but obviously they may sometimes be wanted in a paler version. The answer is not to water them down; what is needed is extender base, the thickened base to which the colour is added in the first place. A tiny amount of colour can be added to the extender base, thus making a paler colour while keeping the paint thick. The paints can be mixed together to make other colours.

These thickened paints are easy to fix. When the fabric is dry, iron it with an iron set at a suitable heat for the fabric.

This type of fabric paint lies on the surface of the fabric fibres and, when heat-set, the colours are permanent and washable. They are suitable for most fabrics and can be applied with a brush, sponge or rag. They can also be used for printing, using a potato cut or a wooden block on which string or felt might be stuck to create a pattern. All brushes and other utensils should be washed immediately after use.

Various makes of paint are available from art supply shops, or in small jars from hardware stores. If larger

84 *Marks made with fabric paint and a brush or sponge*

quantities are required, it is worth contacting manufacturers of fabric printing supplies, particularly for the extender base.

Fabric dyes

Fabric dyes dissolve completely in water and colour the fabric by chemically combining with the fibre. These dyes are readily available at hardware stores in small quantities for hot or cold water dyeing. Both are suitable for dyeing lengths of material, providing the manufacturer's instructions are followed.

Another use of cold water dyes is for space dyeing, which gives patches of random colour on suitable materials. All that is needed is a plastic tray about 5 cm (2 in) deep, such as a developing dish used by photographers or a seed tray lined with a piece of plastic sheet. Make up the dyes to the manufacturer's instructions, except using a total of about 0.4 litre ($\frac{3}{4}$ pint) of water. Soak the fabrics – a mixture of muslins, organdie and silks could be tried, but not synthetics. Spread them around the edge of the dish and spoon over the dyes; two or three contrasting colours give a good result. The wet fabrics will absorb the colours and they will bleed into each other, making subtle mixes. Leave for 30 minutes before pouring away the dyes and rinsing the fabrics.

Other techniques

Silk dyes

Available on the market, for use with silk only, are dyes from France which are made in the most beautiful colours. These can be applied to the fabric by simply holding a brush containing the dye on the silk, and it will spread evenly until the dye on the brush has been used. If you let the colours run into each other, it can make a really beautiful piece of coloured silk.

Before starting to dye the silk, it should be stretched and pinned onto a frame.

Being a liquid, specific areas of colour cannot be brushed in since the colour bleeds through the silk. If a shape is wanted, a barrier needs to be placed round the area to prevent the colour spreading. This is done by drawing round the shape with gutta, which comes in a tube and is held like a pen to draw the outline. This takes practice to get the right pressure to release the gutta; it must be sufficient to go through the fabric to the wrong side. This can be checked by holding the fabric up to the light. The other vital factor is to make sure that the shape is completely enclosed. If these two points are not observed, the colour will creep under or through to the surrounding areas. It is worth practising the application of the gutta until you are able to draw the lines in one continuous movement, as stops and starts create blobs. Leave the dye for 48 hours and then fix it in a fixing bath, following the manufacturer's instructions.

This dye can also be used for space dyeing, the dyes being diluted as wished.

One fabric which contradicts what has been said about watery dyes bleeding into the fabric is silk organza. The dye can be painted on and the colour stays where it is put.

Transfer dyes

This important group of dyes is for use on synthetic materials. The colours are very strong but can be diluted to give pastels.

These dyes are used in a completely different way. The design is drawn on paper, and then coloured with the dye and left to dry. The design is then placed coloured side down on the fabric and ironed with a hot iron on the back of the paper.

This is the basic principle, but there are a few points to be taken into account. The first is that the colours when heated by the iron are not quite the same as before they are heated, and in some cases there is a significant difference. This means that it is essential to make trial tests before making a final decision. Another colour variation occurs according to the fabric used. If the material is 100% synthetic, such as all-nylon or all-polyester, the colour when transferred will be very much stronger than if the fabric is made from a mixture such as poly-cotton, as only the percentage which is synthetic will react with the dye.

Another colour variation will depend on the paper used for the design. It is better if the surface of the paper is not too absorbent, and a fairly smooth, hard surface is recommended. It should also not be too thick, since the paper absorbs a lot of heat. The iron sometimes needs to be set at a temperature hotter than is normally used for synthetics; again, a test piece should be made. Because the iron is hotter than usual for synthetics, care should be taken that any surrounding material is protected, otherwise the fabric may distort or, worse, melt and stick to the iron. The iron itself should be kept moving evenly over the paper, going well beyond the edges of the design to ensure a smooth transfer of colour.

Finally, because the design is turned over when it is being ironed, the image appears in reverse on the fabric. This needs to be thought about, particularly if a subject such as lettering is being used.

The heat fixes the colour on the fabric and makes it safe to wash.

One of the advantages of this dye is that once the design has been drawn on the paper, it can be repainted and printed as often as required, or until the paper cockles.

It is not always easy to apply a smooth layer of the dye to the paper using a brush. An alternative is to spray the paper, using a mouth diffuser or an air brush. A stippled surface can be very effective, particularly if two colours are used, allowing one colour to dry on the paper before adding the second one. These sheets can be transferred in total, or shapes such as flower petals or leaves can be cut out and ironed onto the fabric individually. The shapes could be overlapped if wished. This gives a clear edge, suitable for quilting or, backed with another piece of material, for trapunto quilting. Very dilute dyes can look almost colourless on the paper, but when ironed onto twinkle nylon can be sufficient to make the fabric shimmer. Trial tests must be made to achieve this result and particular care taken to protect surrounding material from the heat of the iron.

Fabric crayons

There are two kinds of fabric crayon. One is for use on natural fibres such as cotton, silk or wool, also on rayon which, although a man-made fabric, is made from wood pulp. These crayons are used directly on the fabric. They are fixed by covering the design with a piece of absorbent paper, and ironing with the iron set at a heat to suit the fabric.

The second kind of crayons are for use on synthetic fabrics. They are used like transfer dyes, by drawing on paper and transferring the design to the fabric by ironing on the back of the paper, remembering that the design will appear in reverse.

These crayons are convenient to use, but they also have drawbacks. The colours are strong, which is not always wanted, and, being made of wax, the colour sometimes spreads. They are ideal for rubbings, which can be made directly onto the fabric in the case of natural fabrics or onto paper for use on man-made materials. Different-size mesh can be rubbed or the rough textures of walls. When using these crayons on fine materials, it is advisable to handle them lightly.

Water-soluble pencils

In addition, particularly where permanence or washability is not a prime factor, inks and water-soluble pencils may be found useful. The latter have been mentioned before for marking a design on fabric; when used wet, either by wetting the pencil or by wetting the material and gently dissolving the colour onto the fabric, they can be invaluable. The colours can be rubbed with a wet finger to mix them together. The pencils come in a wide range of colours, and, of course, can be used on paper as well.

Different ways to use paints and dyes

One of the best things about the fabric paints and dyes that are on the market today is that they can be kept on a shelf or in a cupboard, and be ready to use when the need arises. All that is necessary to make the whole thing painless are a few simple pieces of equipment such as the following:

1 a plastic egg box in which to mix the paint
2 a stencil brush (these can be found in children's toy shops)
3 a soft, 1 cm ($\frac{1}{2}$ in), flat brush
4 a piece of sponge, preferably natural but synthetic will do
5 an old toothbrush
6 a spring clothes peg
7 a water pot for washing brushes, and one for adding to the paints
8 finally, the pots of fabric paint

There is a whole range of colours to choose from, but most can be mixed from the following:

(a) an orange-red and a blue-red
(b) a green-blue and a purple-blue
(c) a lemon yellow and an egg yolk yellow
(d) black and white
(e) an extra effect can be made by adding a pearlized paint to any of the above

In Chapter 1, reasons are given for choosing two of each of the primary colours (see p. 31).

With all methods, it pays to take time mixing the colours to get the correct one. For instance, if a clear orange is wanted, use an orange-red and a warm yellow, not a lime yellow or a blue-red. If purple is to be mixed, use a blue-red with a purple-blue and so on. Always test the colour on the fabric and let it dry completely; colours usually dry lighter than when wet.

In addition, it is a good idea to keep something suitable

for making stencils. Here I would like to mention a material which is useful, flexible in its use and in its handling, and cheap to buy. It has the appearance of Vilene but is made of polythene, and is sold by carpet shops for use as an underlay. It is firm to handle and easy to cut, and it can even be machined and coloured. Its surface is absorbent and therefore the paint must not be too wet or it would soak through and spoil the effect, but as paints used for stencilling must be thick in order to keep a clean edge, this problem should not arise. Used for stencilling by hand it is very successful, but one student did experience difficulty when using an aerosol can of spray. This particular plastic sheeting has the appearance of a web and is sufficiently see-through to be placed over the design, which can then be traced. It can be cut quite easily with scissors, which means that intricate as well as simple shapes can be cut. The same material can, of course, be used to cut out a shape to use as a template, applying colour round the edges and between shapes.

Stencilling

Stencils can be cut from thin card as well as the plastic material mentioned above. If card is used, it should be brushed with a mixture comprising equal parts of boiled linseed oil and turpentine. Treat both sides of the card and leave it to dry. The alternative is to buy ready-oiled card from an art shop.

The fabric to be stencilled should be smoothed and held in place over a folded pad of material such as an old sheet.

The stencil should be secured in place as it is vital that it does not move while the paint is being applied. It can be held in place quite simply by using masking tape or, in the case of the plastic material, it can be pinned.

The paint can be applied with a stencil brush or with a piece of sponge, tapping the fabric rather than brushing it. For greater control of the paint, spread the colour on a piece of sponge or felt first, and then press the brush onto this to load it. If you are using a piece of synthetic sponge to apply the paint, pressure from your fingers sometimes causes blobs. By holding the sponge in a spring clothes peg, it is easier to control. This same preparation and application can be used to apply paint in a freer way, without the use of stencils, where this is required.

85 *This shows the type of subject where different stippling marks on organza could provide a background for overlapping leaves*

Block printing

The thickened range of paints can be used for block printing. Ends of pieces of wood often have a grain which would print well, or blocks can be made by sticking on felt shapes or string. Spreading the paint on sponge or felt, as in stencilling, and then pressing the block onto the pad to pick up the paint will give an even amount of colour, which can then be pressed onto the fabric. For fine fabrics, the excess paint will be pushed through to the pad below, leaving the right amount for the purpose.

These block prints can be used as a base for a design, for example, using stitching which gradually builds up in intensity, finally incorporating strips of organza, dyed or not, as a thread. The lines could be used for shadow Italian quilting; sometimes one line becomes dominant and could be picked out as a quilting line across the whole piece.

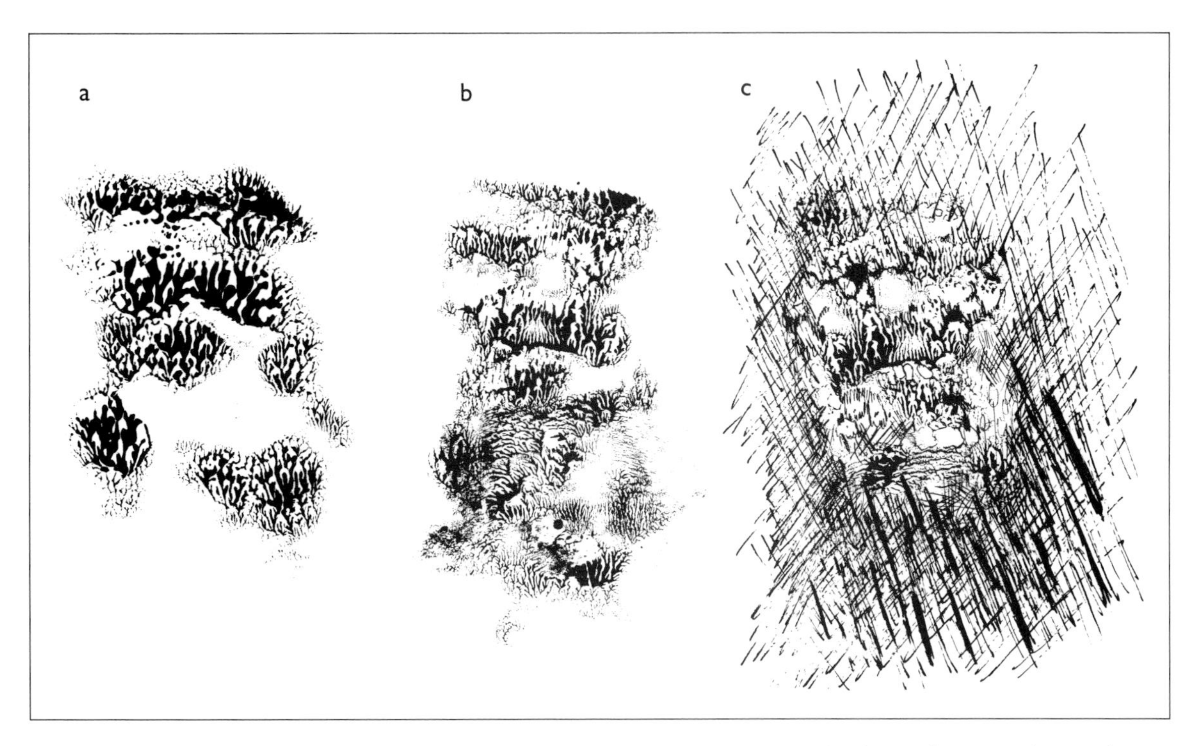

86 a *and* **b** *Prints made by rolling fabric paint between two pieces of plastic sheet, and then pressing the plastic, paint side down, onto paper or fabric*
c *The print could be surrounded by stitching with different thicknesses of thread*

Another printing method which is fun to do and extremely easy is to roll very small amounts of two colours of the thickened paint between two pieces of plastic sheeting. The two pieces of plastic are then pulled apart and each piece is pressed, paint side down, onto the fabric. The two images will be reversed. The colours can be used full strength, or they can be diluted by adding extender base. When this method is used on transparent fabric and this is placed over another material, the effect can be ethereal.

CHAPTER 6

Gathering, Pleating, (Weaving) and Folding

Fine fabrics lend themselves to folding, pleating and gathering as these processes can be done without adding too much bulk. These methods are not only decorative; in some cases, where the transparent fabric might be too fine, tucks, pleats and folds can give a bit more substance while still maintaining a light, flowing quality.

The composition of the materials being used needs to be taken into consideration, as some materials are more springy than others. Fabrics made from natural fibres, such as cotton, silk and rayon, gather and fold beautifully, but are difficult to maintain if the finished item needs washing or ironing. Man-made fabrics such as nylon and polyester are a little more difficult to handle because of their spring, but are much easier to wash and iron and are therefore more applicable to present-day living. Pleats and gathers for clothes and accessories such as bags or hats are the most obvious uses, but these techniques could be used in other ways, for example, on panels or as decorative patches.

Gathering

Gathering is used primarily as a way of controlling fullness, such as in the peasant smocks of the past where a thick, tough garment was the result. When gathering is used on sheer fabrics, the same smocking stitches can produce exquisite decoration for blouses or children's dresses. This chapter, however, will describe other gathering systems which are complete in themselves. These gathers could be used on garments to control fullness on sleeves and yokes, but they can also be used in their own right on panels. By changing the scale, the shadows created will vary while the pattern remains the same. Sections could also be worked in different-coloured fabrics and assembled as a grid.

Careful measuring is required for these gathering techniques, and it is best to mark the fabric before stitching. A suitable marker is one which can be wiped away with a damp cloth when the stitching is finished. Another essential thing to remember when gathering is to fasten the thread really well; it can be extremely frustrating to gather material carefully, only to have the thread pull through. Use a strong thread, as there is quite a resistance when the thread is pulled. A strong thread does not mean a thick one; a polyester or nylon thread matching the fabric in colour would be best. The matching colour is necessary as the thread will stay in the gathers, unlike smocking where the gathering thread is removed once the decorative stitches have been worked across the folds.

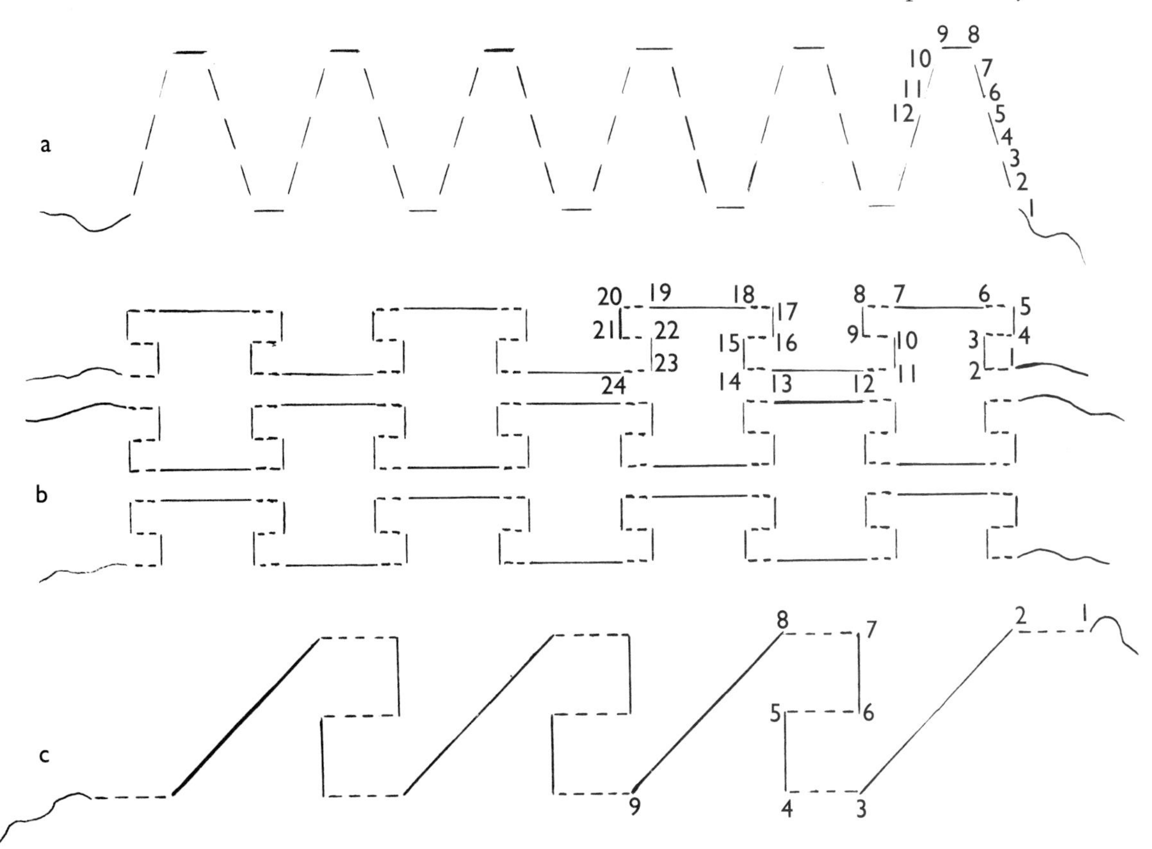

87 *The sequence of stitching for three different ways of gathering. The needle enters the fabric on the odd numbers and emerges on the even numbers.* **a** *is illustrated in Fig. 88,* **b** *in Fig. 89 and* **c** *in Fig. 90*

The decorative gathering methods are shown in Figs. 87a–c. They are very suitable for fine materials as

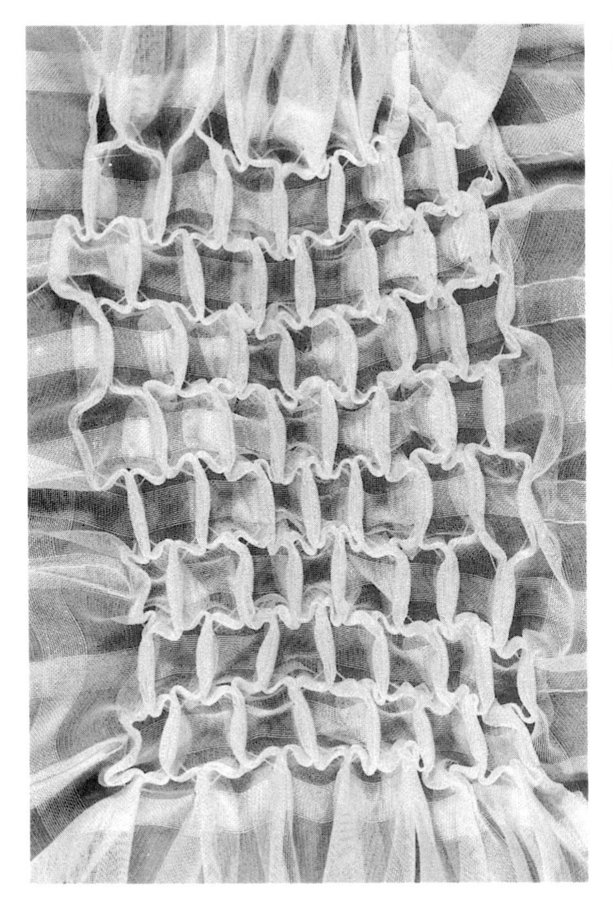

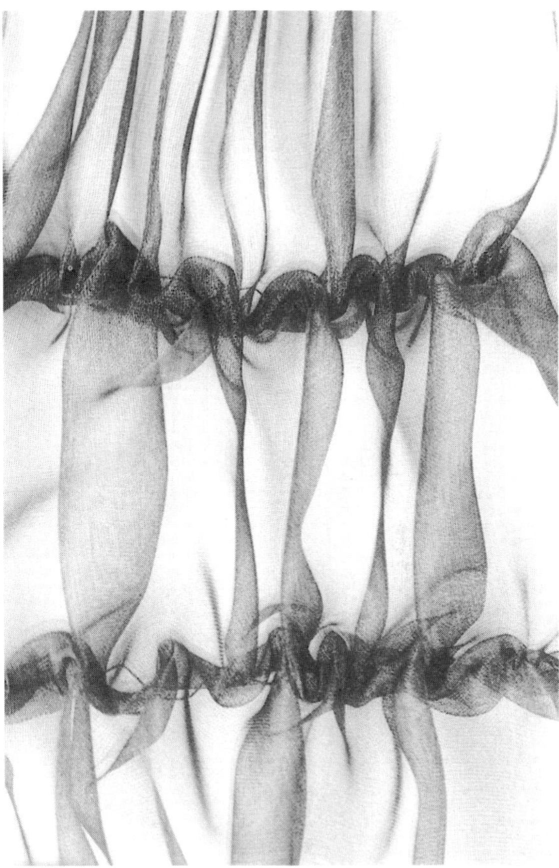

89 *A shadow-striped material was used for this sample, which uses the gathering sequence shown in Fig. 87b (Peggy Cronin)*

90 *A black nylon organza was used for this sample, which features the gathering sequence shown in Fig. 87c*

88 *Various stages of pulling the gathering thread, following Fig. 87a*

they use about four times the finished width, for example, 100 cm (40 in) gathers to a finished width of 25 cm (10 in). Of course, a trial sample should always be worked where measurement is critical.

Variation

Two layers of transparent fabrics gathered as one will add substance to the gathered folds, as well as causing beautiful colour effects between the two fabrics.

Suffolk puffs

Suffolk puffs can look very pretty worked in fine fabric. This is another gathering variation, sometimes called yo-yo patchwork. If used as separate units and made in delicate fabrics, the puffs can be made quite tiny and used to decorate many items, from a bridal veil or a little bridesmaid's bag to boxes or panels.

First make a template from thin card. Cut a circle, the radius of which is the size of the finished puff plus $\frac{1}{2}$ cm ($\frac{1}{4}$ in)

91 *The same sequence as in Fig. 87a, but with more gathering lines (Joan Beasant)*

92 *Suffolk puffs made with organzas and fine silk habotai*

for a turning, then cut a second template the same size. It is much easier to cut a small circle from thin fabric if you hold the material firmly sandwiched between the two card discs. Using this method, cut out a circle of material. Fold over the turning and, using a matching thread, fasten on very securely. Work a line of small running stitches near to the fold, pull the thread tight and fasten off.

These little puffs can be stitched down with the gathered side or the plain side uppermost. Secure them with just a French knot in the middle, or hold a section down with a group of knots, seeding or any other suitable stitch.

Variations

1 If you do not turn under a hem, the gathering can be made at any distance from the edge. When the thread is pulled up, a flower-like shape is the result.
2 Using the above variation, and then fraying the edges, gives the appearance of a shaggy-petalled flower. If the correct pink is used, the puffs will resemble pinks or carnations.

Pleating

Pleating is another way of controlling fullness and is usually associated with dressmaking. However, the play of light on pleats, particularly when the material is shot nylon organza, makes it a method worthy of consideration for use on panels or hangings. Again, if two layers are used, the colour effects can be quite stunning. You can change the size of the pleats and stitch squares of them together like patches, changing the direction of the pleats as in a chequerboard; this design could be used for cushions. The fact that such exotic effects can be made using both easy-care and hard-wearing materials opens up a whole new way of looking at interior design.

Weaving

Weaving transparent materials is another way to exploit their ability to change tones of colours when one fabric crosses another. By cutting strips of various widths and colours, weaving can be used to form a grid, either regular or irregular. This could be used as a base for a panel to be worked by hand, or machined onto a background piece of

93 *Edges of pleats, or deep tucks, can be stitched along an irregular line. Cut the fabric back to this line, then cover it with satin stitch*

94 *Irregular tucks, stitched across the bias*

95 *The same treatment as Fig. 94, but by pulling across the opposite direction 3D effects can be made*

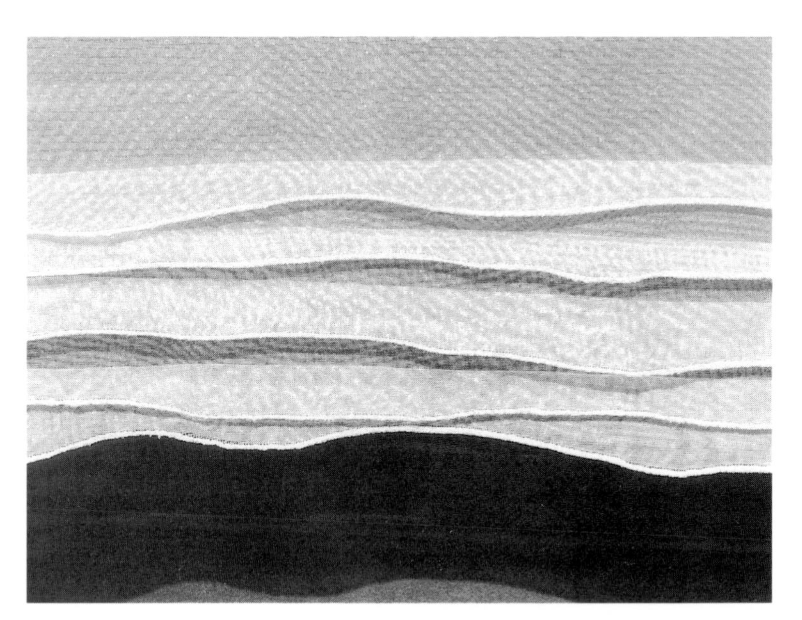

material, with further machining added. Some of the grid ideas from Chapter 1 would be appropriate for this (see p. 30).

If raw edges are not suitable, the bias binder maker previously mentioned (p. 52) could be used. Although this little gadget is for making bias strips, it will also turn under the edges of fabric strips cut on the straight. It can be used to make much narrower strips, as the basic-width strip can be folded edge to edge and ironed along the centre; with fine materials, this can be done without the finished strip being too bulky. These narrow strips can then be used for intricate patterns such as those found on Celtic crosses, or for plaiting.

To use the bias binder maker in this way, cut a strip of fabric about 2.5 cm (1 in) wide, either on the bias or on the straight. If you cut one end to a point, you can feed it into one side of the little gadget and it will come out with the sides turned over, ready to be ironed in place.

Variations

If you feed about a 1.5 cm ($\frac{1}{2}$ in) strip of iron-on web, such as the one used for turning up hems, in with the fabric strip, this will seal the edges of the fabric strip and create a firm strip of fabric with the edges turned under, ideal for weaving. It would be advisable to cover the strip with non-stick paper before ironing in order to protect the iron.

Bias strips of transparent fabrics, whether with raw or with neatened edges, can be used for wrapping, for instance round a fine core of soft wadding or string. This technique could be used for edges, or for stems or branches on a panel, or these themselves could be woven.

Folding

Decorating edges with folded triangles is a method known to dressmakers and embroiderers alike, and using transparent fabrics for this purpose is a pretty way to finish the edges of a baby's dress or the hem and sleeves of a christening robe. If you use a fine fabric, tiny points can be made, suitable to the scale of such a garment. Similarly, small bridesmaids' dresses or little bags could be embellished. Fig. 96 shows how these points are constructed. Again, by using two layers of different-coloured materials, two-toned effects can be made.

96 *Folded points:*

a *Fold the square along the line AB*

b *Fold the triangle along the dotted line*

c *A meets B*

d *Assemble the triangles as shown in the diagram, and stitch a line through all the layers to hold them together*

(Second method)

a *Fold the square along the dotted line AB*

b *Fold so that A meets C and B meets C*

c *Overlap the triangles at the bottom and make a line of stitching through all the layers*

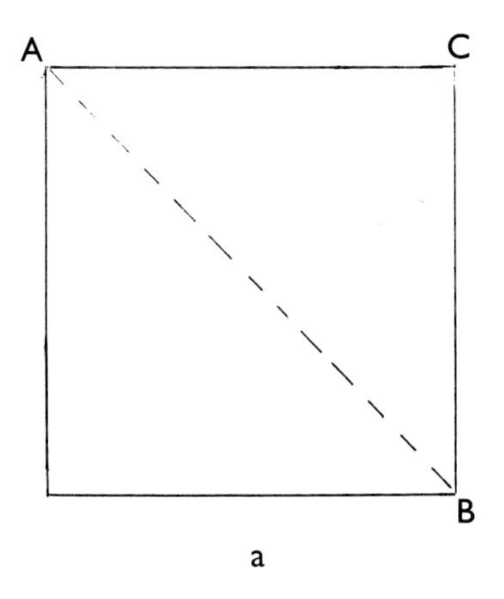

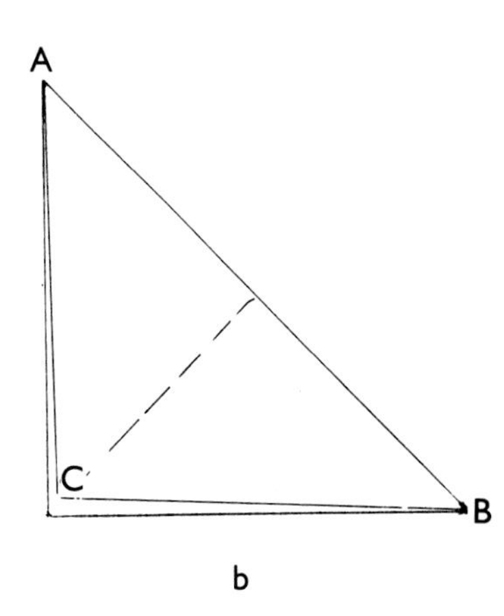

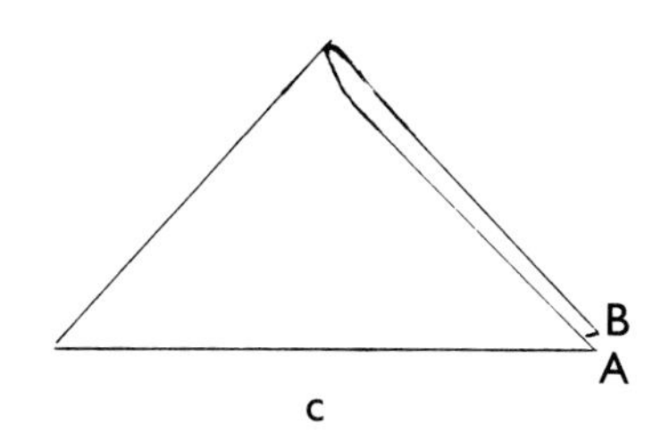

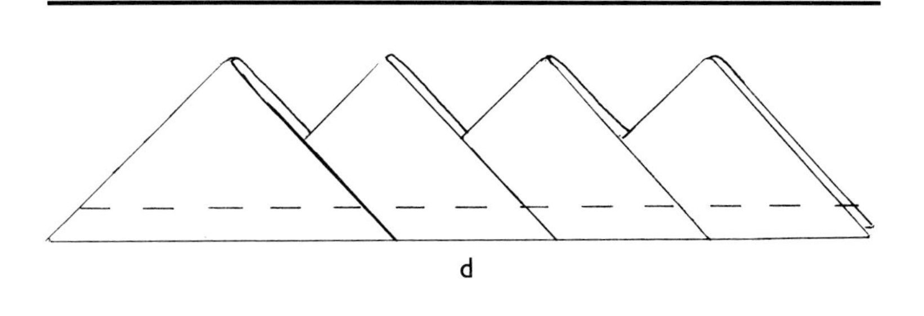

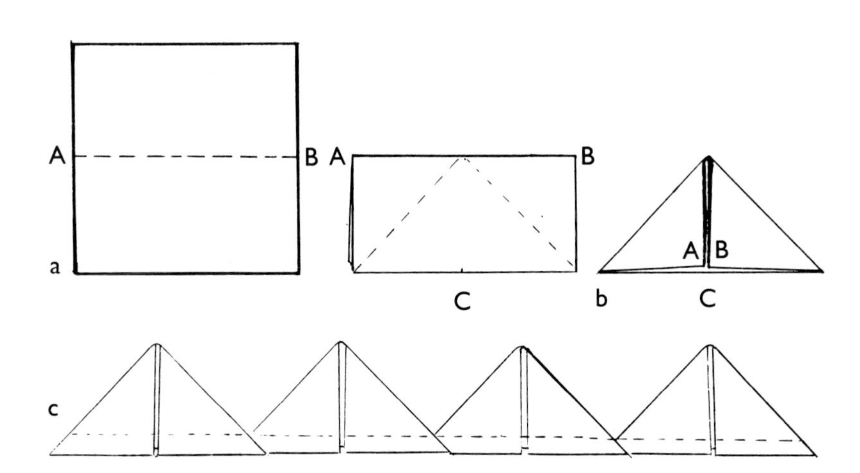

97 *Folded organza squares, with coloured organza centres (Edwina Rogers)*

Variations

1 A piece of lace could be folded in with the second method (Fig. 96).
2 The top half of the square could be coloured, to show a coloured lining when folded.
3 The points could be machine embroidered.

Another folding technique suitable for transparent fabric is cathedral patchwork. By using the first part of the folding process and different-sized squares, a panel based on a grid can be constructed. The patches could be joined together in the usual way, or attached just at the corners.

CHAPTER 7

Textures

Many of the fine fabrics mentioned so far are prized for their smoothness and sheen, and are therefore not thought of as having very much texture. This is true if we consider surface texture only, but the fineness and fluidity of these materials, coupled in some instances with toughness, means that they can be manipulated in various ways to create a good deal of surface interest and texture. With man-made fabrics such as nylons and the polyesters, the strength and the spring of the fibres can be used, whereas in the case of soft silk or cotton muslins their ability to flow and mould adds another dimension.

Checking the fabric

Before using any fabric, it is useful to carry out a few tests to check its characteristics. For instance, does it tear easily, does it fray at the slightest touch or does the edge remain firm? Does it scorch at a high or a low temperature, and when burnt does it flame or merely melt? Fabrics are made from so many different mixtures these days that it is sometimes better to know how they behave than what they are made from.

OVERLEAF

98 *(left) Strips of fabric looped and worked in tent stitch on rug canvas (Margaret Maple)*

99 *(right) The felt base of this sample was covered with Bondaweb. A variety of small pieces of transparent fabrics were ironed on, and diagonal lines of machining worked on top. Beads and French knots were added (Caroline Harland)*

Fraying

Fraying fabrics often dilutes the colour at the edges. With shot fabrics, the two colours of the warp and the weft can be shown. If you cut the fabric on the bias, a whole line of thread cannot be removed; instead, as short amounts fray

100 a A strip of organza cut and frayed on the bias
b Silk organza tangling as it frays
c Frayed black nylon organza

along the warp or weft, the threads begin to tangle together in a way that suggests the texture of hedgerows in winter, particularly if black nylon organza is used.

An extension of this idea is to have a number of layers; any number from two upwards which will fit under the foot of the machine is permissible. Stitch with a straight stitch across the bias, making stripes with the stitching about 1 cm ($\frac{1}{2}$ in) between. Then slash through the layers on the bias between the stitching, but *not* through the bottom layer. Ruffle the raw edges. (You can even put them in the washing machine to ruffle them further.) This can create a very rich textured surface if many layers are used, or a lightly ruffled surface if you use one or two layers.

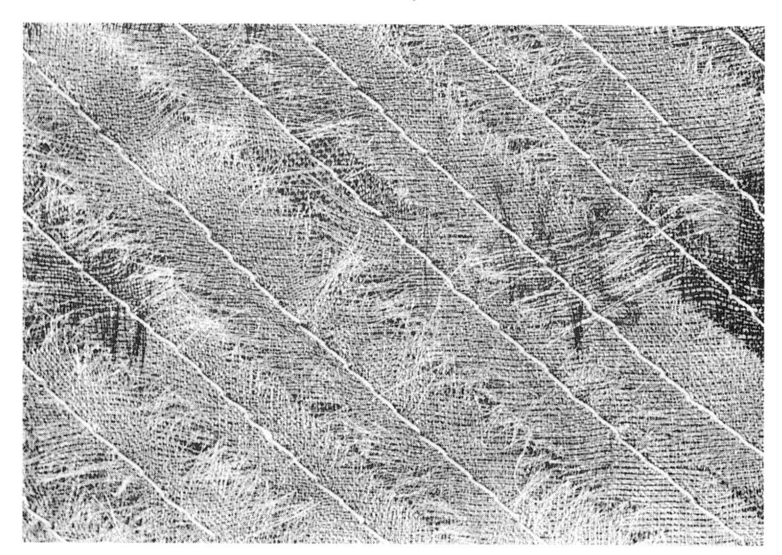

101 a *Layers stitched together across the bias, about 1 cm ($\frac{1}{2}$ in) apart. The layers are cut through to (but not right through) the bottom layer, and then frayed*

b *Many more layers are used, giving a much thicker and richer result (Joan Beasant)*

102 *Dyed silk chiffons, cut into strips and used as a thread to make French knots and long straight stitches*

Using fabric strips as thread

Cutting gauzes or muslins into narrow strips and using them as a thread is a very satisfying way of making a texture. In this case, the fabric should be cut with the grain, not across the bias as this would make a thread too weak to stitch with. Following the rule that the needle should make the way for the thread, choose a suitable-sized needle and in this way it will be possible to stitch on quite fine materials. This method can be worked on other backgrounds such as wool or hessian with success.

French knots, cross stitch, in fact most stitches are suitable, but stitches such as raised chain band which are

OPPOSITE
103 *Using strips of fabric as a thread to work raised chain band and looped couching, to give another interpretation of delphiniums*

formed on bars give a very textured look worked with fabric strips. Stitches can be used for texture alone, contrasting textured areas with smooth ones in a pattern, or in a more interpretive way such as for a garden or hedgerow, particularly for spiky subjects like delphiniums or gladioli. Looped and pendant couching are also successful, with a strip of fabric looped and couched down in place of a thread.

Wrapping stitches or loops such as buttonhole loops, or working detached buttonhole stitch with a length of fine organza, are other possibilities which could lead to exciting surfaces, contrasting perhaps with smooth, uncluttered areas.

Textures using the machine

Using the machine to create bumpy, textured areas can be fun to do and gives the opportunity to indulge in the way the jewel-like colours of the organzas sparkle when their surfaces are ruffled. When this is combined with some of the exotic gold and lustre threads made for the machine, you

104 *Rich textured surfaces can be made by laying fine chiffons over thicker fabrics, such as felts and velvets, and then machining through all the layers*

can create very rich surfaces indeed. Jewellery from Ancient Egypt or the Baroque period is a good source of ideas for this type of texture.

Strips of fabric, gathered on the machine, could be the start of garden or landscape textures. Choose suitable colours, for instance, for a garden, choose colours from flowers or for a rough track in a country landscape choose

105 *Paths or cobbles made by covering blocks of wadding with very fine black chiffon and machining between*

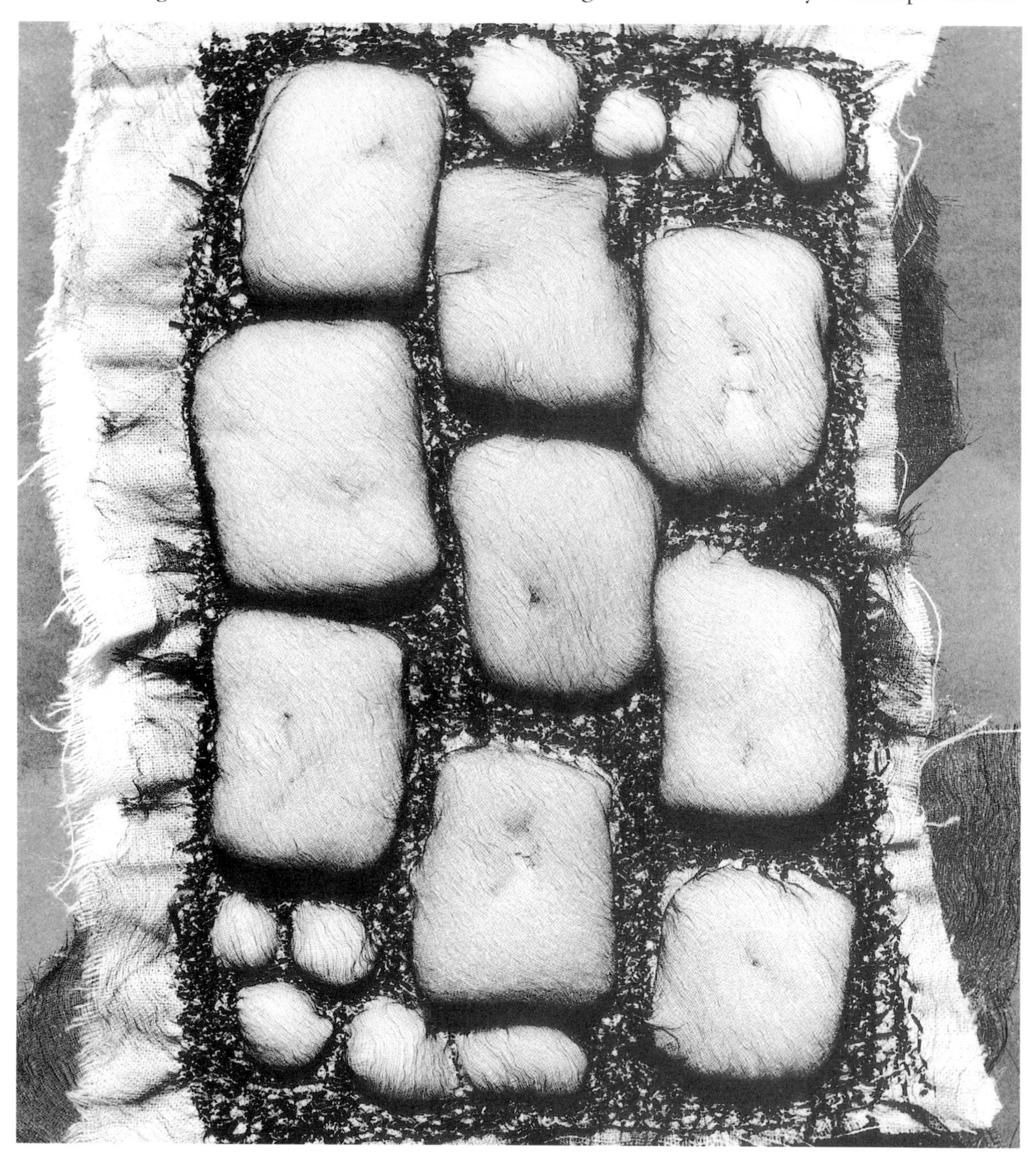

106 *Handmade paper was covered with shot silk and chiffon, and machined using a twin needle. The piece was then cut into strips and machined together again. It was mounted over rolls of felt (Penny Lawes)*

greys and browns, and cut strips about 2 cm ($\frac{3}{4}$ in) wide. Use a matching thread top and bottom, and fasten the threads securely by stitching and reversing for one or two stitches. Using a long stitch setting, machine down the centre of the first strip of fabric. Remove the strip from the machine and pull one of the threads to gather the strip. Do not cut off the end of the thread. If a number of strips are to be gathered, it is easier if the lines of stitching are made on a piece of fabric before cutting it into strips.

Thread a needle with the thread on the strip, and make a back stitch to secure the gathers. Using the same thread, attach the gathered strip to the background fabric, which should be mounted tightly in an embroidery hoop. Using the free machining setting, machine over and around the gathered piece, flattening some areas and leaving others alone. It may be necessary to use a zigzag.

CHAPTER 8

Finished pieces

How many ideas develop to fruition, and how many flounder along the way, through lack of will or just sheer lack of time? Many good ideas fail because they are not pursued beyond the obvious, resulting in a feeling of dissatisfaction and lost opportunity. Certainly, every piece of work has problems to be solved; indeed, embroidery as a whole is a problem-solving process, which may surprise many people. From the simple choice of which fabric to use with which thread, there are decisions to be made. This chapter will follow some items through from start to finish, using transparent or fine fabrics and some of the techniques already described.

Planning and making a wedding dress

The wedding dress was probably the largest project I have ever undertaken, with moments of desperation finally justified by the moment of elation when my daughter-in-law appeared on her wedding day. As I had this book in mind, the fabric had to be transparent. With this one stipulation, we discussed her preferences for the style. Her choice was for a short twenties-style dress, and, after one or two joint sketches, she left it entirely to me, which was very generous.

I found that I needed a theme and, as she had been born in Canada, I thought the maple leaf would offer me scope and would please her, which it did. It is not always necessary to have an involved or clever idea; a good fundamental shape offers unlimited possibilities for development.

107 *Sketches for the wedding dress:*
a *The front view*
b *The back view showing the train, with a few Bramley apples among the leaves*

First trials

One or two tentative ideas were carried out on the machine, the original plan being to use silk organza over white silk habotai. The leaf shape was stitched through both layers of silk, and the top layer of organza cut away to show the silk habotai. The next trial was to colour the bottom layer a very, very pale pink, which would show through when the organza layer was cut away.

The other sample used silk muslin, with free machine embroidery over the leaf shape; this would float over a foundation dress of cream silk.

At this point, a choice had to be made whether to use white or cream. Individual skin tones seem to look better with either white or cream, but rarely with both. Cream was chosen, and it was decided to use silk muslin floating over pale cream silk. This in turn influenced the design, which was to keep everything soft and flowing.

Developing the embroidery design

Having decided to use the maple leaf as a theme, photographs were taken to see how the leaves grow and place themselves on the branch. To give variation to the design, four different sizes were used.

This is where a camera can be a useful tool, particularly if a projector is available. By projecting different sizes onto drawing paper, outlines of leaves can be made. Another method is to make rubbings of the back of four different-sized leaves, and this was the method I used.

I cut out several paper leaves and arranged them on a copy of the bodice pattern, which I had drawn out on a large sheet of paper. When a satisfactory arrangement had been made, I drew round the leaves to make a full-size guide of where the embroidery would be placed. As the edge of the bodice was to hang loose, with the leaves forming an irregular line, care had to be taken that there were no gaps left between the leaves along this edge.

Putting the design into practice

The idea of tacking or drawing out the design on such fine material was not only daunting, but could have marked the fabric. However, the paper pattern did need to be marked out on the silk muslin, as the embroidery was to be worked before the dress pieces were cut out. This was done with a water-soluble pen marker, allowing a margin of about 4 cm (2 in). This margin is advisable for two reasons, one being that any embroidery slightly tightens a fabric, and secondly the blue mark of the pen would not need to be removed.

To define the leaf shapes to be embroidered, four different-sized stencils were cut from under-carpet polythene sheeting (see p. 93). Each time a leaf was to be embroidered, the stencil was placed under the framed fabric and the embroidery worked within the shape. It was found easier to see one leaf in relation to another if the stencil was placed under the transparent fabric rather than on top. The four stencils were soft and flexible, so they lasted for the whole of the embroidery; as about 350 leaves were worked, it can be assumed to be a successful method.

One of the biggest problems to be overcome was stretching this fine fabric in a hoop. The silk muslin was so

108 *This photograph illustrates the subtle way leaves change direction to reach the light*

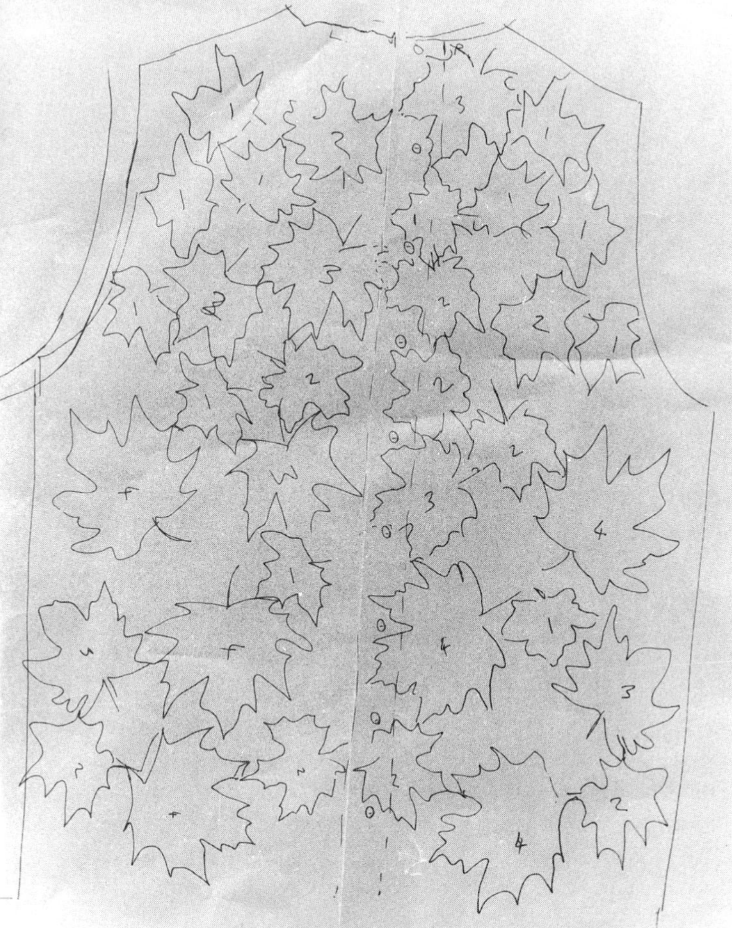

109 *Marking out the wedding dress bodice pattern with the different-sized leaves*

110 *Part of the top layer of the bodice, showing the cut edge*

delicate that trying to stretch it in a wooden hoop caused the fabric to split, even when the inside ring was bound. The solution for this problem has been described in Chapter 4 (see p. 71). Briefly, two circles of cotton fabric were cut to fit the hoop, and the centres were cut out and discarded. The muslin was sandwiched between these cotton rings and these took the strain during the stretching.

Various threads were tried, but in the end a one-ply silk cream thread and an ivory machine embroidery thread were chosen for the bodice. These threads gave a slight difference in texture and colour, but kept a harmony between the fabric and the embroidery suitable for the purpose.

The sleeves were not to have a base of cream silk, and so these were made of two layers of muslin, the top layer being shorter than the bottom one.

Following the maple leaf theme, and the glorious colours of the Canadian fall, it was decided to bring these colours into the skirt, but in a pastel range. Rayon threads were used for this, in cream, peach and a variegated thread. Again, the edges were to be cut away following the edges of the leaves, therefore all the leaves had to touch.

The train was made separately and fastened on with studs at the hipline. As a gesture to my son, five pale green Bramley apples were slipped in amongst the leaves.

Embroidery for dress has many pitfalls, but, with care and regard for the occasion for which it is being worked, it can be great fun to do.

111 *The double layer of the sleeve on the wedding dress*

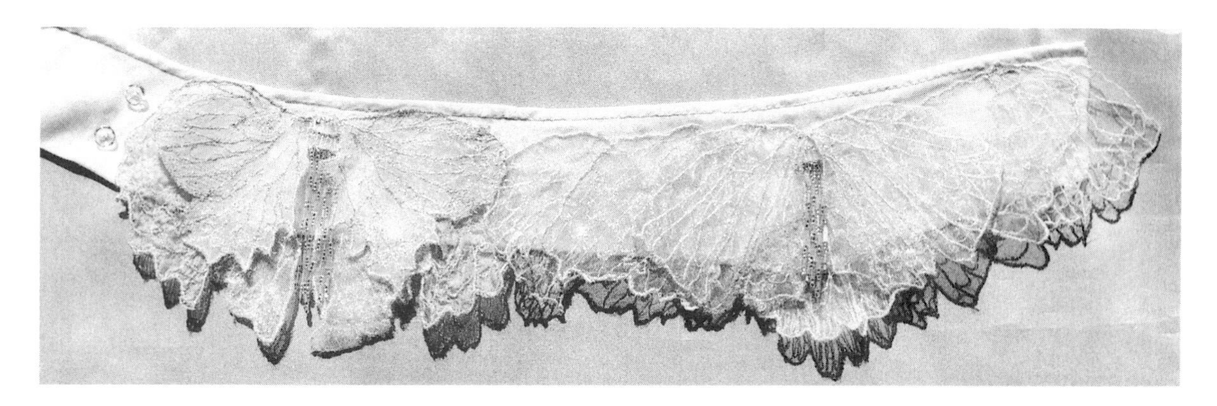

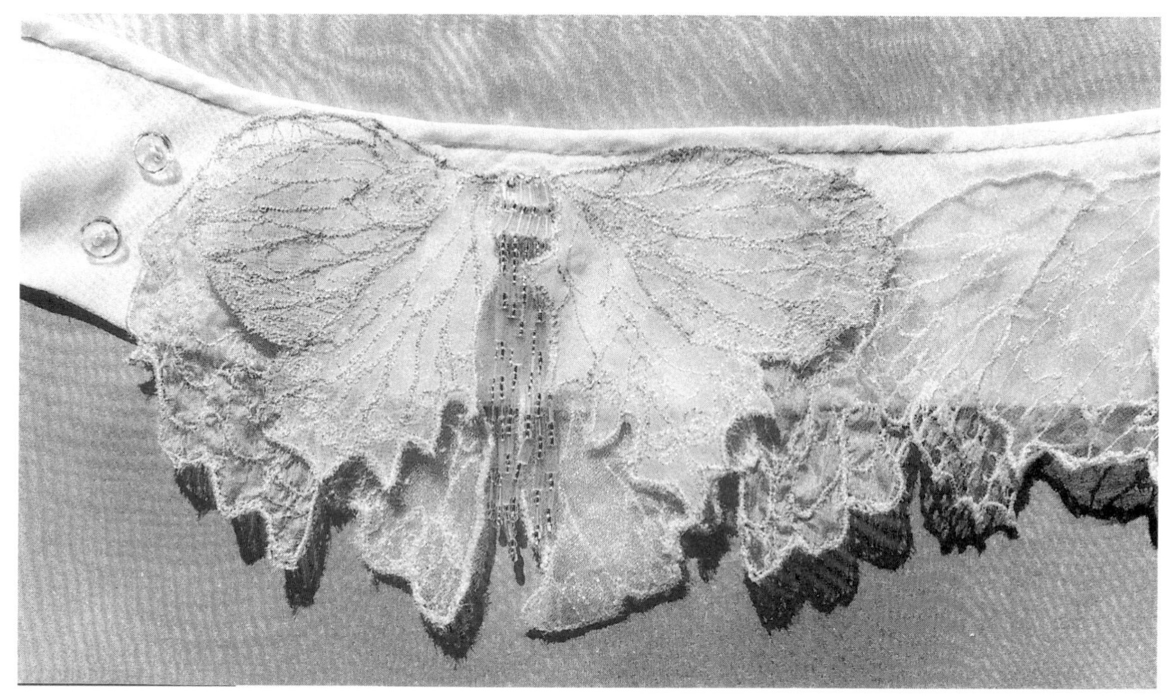

112 a *A collar, worked on the machine, using crystal organzas and beads. The design is based on a moth (Monica Harris)*
b *A detail of the embroidery*

Waistcoats

Waistcoats lend themselves to embroidery, probably better than any other garment. As non-essential pieces of clothing, they can be used as accessories and decorated with many different embroidery techniques.

Before working out a design, certain questions need to be answered. Why is the garment being made? Is it for warmth or as a decorative accessory? Obviously the answer to this question would influence the choice of materials. We do not usually associate transparent materials with warmth, but in fact the richly coloured nylon organzas look very good applied with machine satin stitch to felt, in particular to

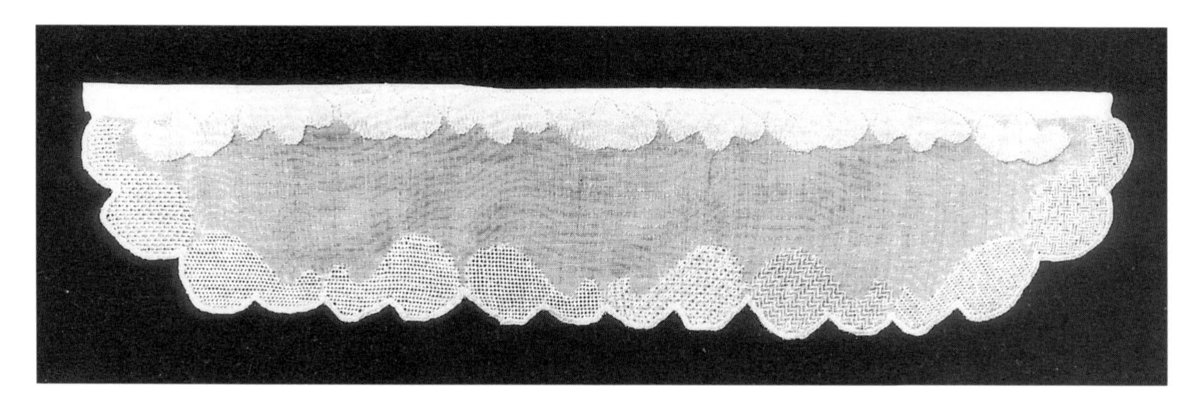

113 a *A collar worked on very fine muslin, using shadow work and pulled work (Suzanne Evans)*
b *A detail of the pulled work*

handmade felt. The stitching flattens the felt, giving a quilted look. These nylon organzas often look better used in small or broken areas.

Silk wadding is available from certain specialist suppliers (see p. 142). Used with fine silk, plus appliqué or reverse appliqué, this is a good combination, maintaining the lightness of the fabrics with warmth.

Where warmth is not a priority, many of the techniques for transparent fabrics could be used. One in particular is the shadow appliqué shown in the cyclamen photograph (Fig. 51). The background fabric does not have to be transparent; the top one does, of course, but the advantage of this technique is that there are no raw edges and the finished embroidery is pliable.

Table mats

The table mat used the same technique, but, instead of being worked by hand using pin stitch, the stitching was done on

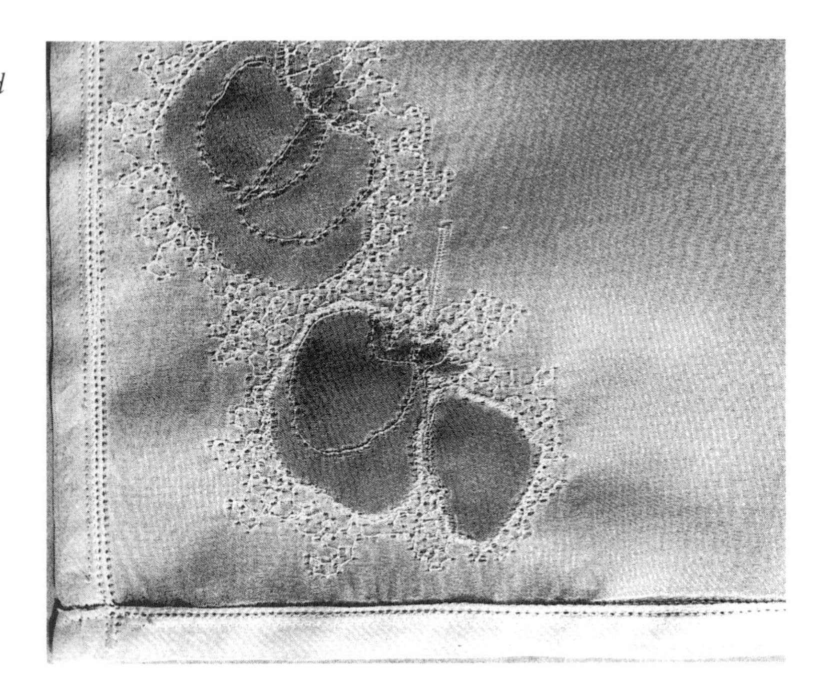

114 *A corner of a table mat, showing shadow appliqué and free machining using the hem stitch needle*

115 *A drawing from the edge of a dandelion leaf*

the machine using a hem stitch needle. You could design a different flower for each table mat, more interesting than repeating the same one.

For the table mat shown, a sweet pea was chosen. The first thing to be decided was the size, and 2 cm (1 in) was added for turnings. As a small turning would have shown through, the first turn and the second turn were the same width. The second layer of fabric was cut to measure the finished size of the mat, as this was held within the hem.

Before stitching the hem, the flower shape was sandwiched in between the two layers and held in place with a tacking stitch. The two layers were then stretched in an embroidery hoop and free machined, using a hem stitch needle. Where this is not possible, an ordinary machine needle could be used. (A word of caution: when making a mat such as this, care should be taken to make sure that the right side is uppermost and not the hem side.) Finally, the hem was tacked down and machined, using the hem stitch

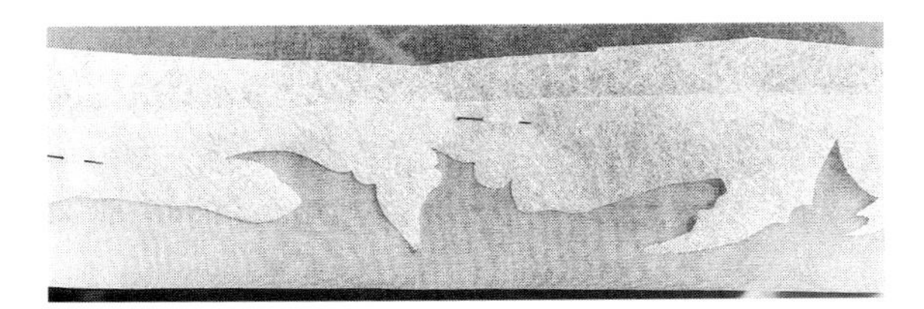

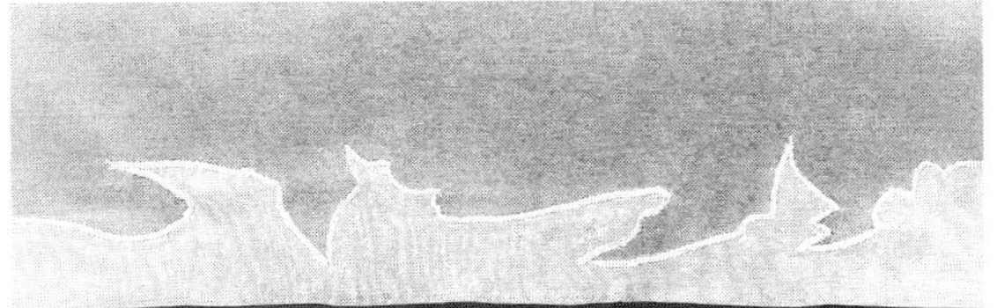

116 a *A pattern cut from the polythene sheeting used under carpets. The design was taken from the leaf drawing in Fig. 115. The pattern is shown pinned in position, before being machined round the edge*
b *After working a line of straight stitch machining cut away the excess hem material, and finish the edge with satin stitch*

needle. Again, if a hem stitch needle is not available, a straight stitch could be used. Alternatively, the hem could be hem stitched or pin stitched by hand.

Cushions

Cushions can be plain and purely practical, for comfort, or used as an accent point of interest in a room. They are a

117 *A kaftan made from crystal organzas. It could also be used as a wallhanging (Ros Chilcot)*

118 *A hat made from handmade felt and organza (Virginia Epstein)*

perfect vehicle for the embroiderer to display both her art and her craft. Transparent fabrics and some of the techniques described can be used on cushions with great effect and still be practical.

The design needs to be chosen carefully; it would be inappropriate to have a flowery design in an ultra high-tech room, and vice versa. Having decided on the type of design,

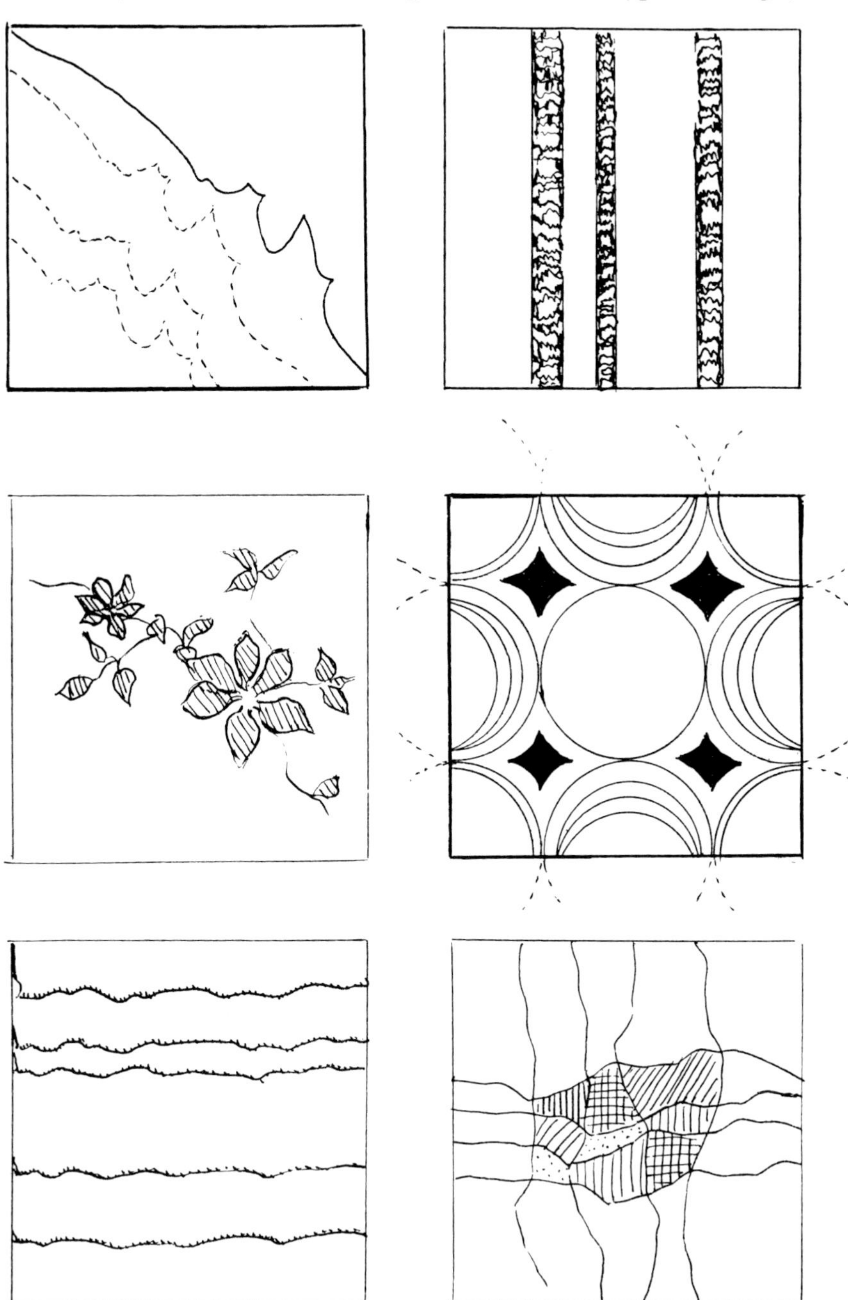

119 *Various ideas for cushions*

120 *A boa, made of chiffons and georgette (Marion Norberg)*

121 *A smocked bag made from gold lurex fabric covered with cream-coloured georgette, the two fabrics worked together as one (Doreen Plews)*

let us say geometric, then you could use one based on a grid or created with mirrors, as explained in Chapter 1. If a more abstract design is decided upon, an interesting line theme could be developed (see p. 21).

A boa

To show that we need not take ourselves too seriously, Fig. 120 shows a boa made for fun by Marion Norberg in San Francisco for Constance Howard in 1986. It is based on a seaweed shape which is stitched upside down to a tape, allowing the soft 'fronds' to bend and drape.

CHAPTER 9

Panels

122 *This panel was worked on the machine, using nets and other fine materials, including water-soluble fabric (Penny Lawes)*

The appeal of embroidery generally is that it is suitable for all kinds of projects, whether as decoration for practical items or as a method of expressing ideas, as a painter or a sculptor would. On a panel or hanging, embroidery must stand or fall on its own merit; it is not a decoration for anything, but a work in its own right.

There is no magic formula for success, but it helps if you have an idea, whether it be a group of shapes or colours which stir the emotions and will not go away. However simple the idea, it should inspire a personal drive tc interpret the idea using fabric and thread.

Everyone approaches a piece of work in a different way. One person may like to have everything worked out to the last detail before starting work; another might prefer a freer approach, with a few trial samples, allowing the embroidery to develop within a general framework. Often the embroid-

123 *This piece of work uses fine handmade felt with appliqué and machine embroidery (Amanda Clayton)*

124 *Overlapping transparent fabrics were stitched with straight horizontal stitches to portray water along a riverbank*

ery technique itself will influence which of these methods is chosen. I would certainly recommend the second approach when using transparent fabrics, as so often the result of one fabric falling on another can alter one's ideas or suggest alternatives.

Whether you are working a figurative piece of work or a more abstract one, it is worth planning the general tonal range. With transparent fabrics, this can be done by overlapping shapes or by covering them with a larger piece, as if applying a glaze over a painting. Where the fabrics overlap can give intense points of colour, and from two or three fabrics many other densities can be made.

Personally, I find more and more that I use two layers of fabric, sometimes cutting away the top layer to reveal the bottom one, sometimes stitching on the bottom layer and on both sides of the top layer to give the impression of depth. There are times when colour is needed but no texture, and even the finest thread will create a texture. This can happen, for instance, in the distance of a landscape. The colour in this case can be applied with a wash of fabric dye or, if this is inappropriate, layers of transparent fabrics might be used.

Using transparent fabrics does not mean that a whole panel must be made from those fabrics and none other. As with any creative piece of work, it is a matter of choosing the right material for interpretation. In some cases, just small amounts are required in certain areas.

It might be useful to explain where and why transparent fabrics have been used in some of the illustrations shown.

'View over the Channel'

In 'View over the Channel', which is the view from where I live, there is a 25-mile stretch of water which on occasions

125 *Organzas can be used successfully for windows (Caroline Harland)*

126 The photograph of bracken was a useful reference when working the panel 'Autumn Mists'

reflects spectacular sunsets. This view influences me considerably. The sky in the panel was made by gradually adding layers of crystal organzas to deepen the colour from pale lemon to deep pink. The lemon crossing the pink made the gradation of colour. The water was covered with grey organza which gave a sparkle. Over this, clouds and reflections were worked with metal threads and gold and silver kid.

'Autumn Mists'

In the panel 'Autumn Mists', the problem was to show the profusion of the bracken in the foreground, but also to create the feeling of autumn mistiness. Any stitching for the distance, however fine, on the same layer of fabric as the bracken would not have given me the atmosphere I wanted. I solved the problem by stitching a background of woodland and covering it with the bracken-stitched layer of organza. Before stitching the bracken, the lower part of the organza was stippled with earthy colours to give greater depth.

127 A background layer was worked for the panel 'Autumn Mists'

128 *A double layer of organza gives the suggestion of water in the distance. A number of layers of different materials, including transparent ones, were used for the foreground*

'Viewpoint'

For the panel 'Viewpoint', I wished to focus interest through the hole in the wire netting. This is an instance where a notebook or photographs prove useful. The wire netting did not conveniently appear in front of this view. It was a broken fence on a car park; I thought it had possibilities, so I photographed it and filed it away. When I was contemplating working the view, I remembered the hole in the fence and thought it would give added interest. The background fabric was lightly dyed to show the fields and heather. The fence was projected the right size onto a sheet of acetate, and drawn very carefully as all the ends needed to connect properly. The acetate sheet was then placed over the dyed background, to find a suitable position and to check the size.

Organza was placed over the acetate and the lines of the fence were traced onto it, using a well-sharpened grey watercolour pencil.

Wishing to focus round the hole, I used whip stitch, starting a little way in from the edges, the grey pencil drawing being left for the rest. I tried to follow each strand of wire through the tangle, which gave quite a texture to the surface, making sure that the edge around the hole was completely covered by the whip stitch. The view on the background, seen through the hole, was then worked on the machine. When embroidering with the machine, it is a great temptation to continue with the same thread in the bobbin. To stop myself from doing this, I deliberately put only about

129 *Muslins, dyed and cut into strips and used as threads, are some of the ways transparent fabrics have been used to interpret the feeling of summer profusion*

130 *This panel used the machine for stitching and gathering, and for making individual flowers*

131 *Ferns, using fishbone stitch, on a lightly dyed green background of silk organza. The back of the stitch can be seen, as well as the front. The sample using the hem stitch needle is lying behind it*

4 m ($4\frac{1}{2}$ yd) of one colour in the bobbin at a time. This way I kept a variation in the heather colours which gave added subtlety.

The background view was laced over card. Then the netting layer was placed in position with a few holding stitches round the 'hole', which at this stage had not been cut away. This layer was laced across the back and finally, and very carefully, the 'hole' was removed.

The way one person uses these fine materials will differ from the way another embroiderer will, and the range of possibilities keeps growing. For a final proof of the way ideas can constantly surprise, now, as I finish this book, I have just seen the stitch sample of leaves sitting on top of the machine hem stitch sample which I had not thought of using as a background before.

Bibliography

Embroidery Backgrounds – Painting and Dyeing Techniques, Pauline Brown, Batsford, 1984

Pattern Design, Lewis F. Day, Taplinger Publishing Company, 1979

Embroidery and Colour, Constance Howard, Batsford, 1976

The Elements of Colour, Johannes Itten, Van Nostrand Reinhold Company, 1970

Machine Embroidery – Lace and See-through Techniques, Moyra McNeill, Batsford, 1985

Needlework School, Practical Study Group, QED, 1984

Suppliers

UK

Borovick Fabrics Ltd
16 Berwick Street
London W1
A wide range of organzas and exotic fabrics

Campden Needlecraft Centre
High Street
Chipping Campden
Gloucestershire
Silk organza; Orient Express dyes for use on silk

George Rowney & Co. Ltd
P.O. Box 10
Bracknell
Berkshire RG12 4ST
Screen and fabric paints

Sericol Group Ltd
24 Parsons Green Lane
London SW6 4HT
(Also branches in Bristol, Birmingham, Liverpool, Manchester, Newcastle and Glasgow)
Texiscreen TS inks (for fabrics) (minimum supplied 1 litre)

UK

Sue Harris
The Mill
Tregoyd Mill
Three Cocks
Brecon
Powys LD3 0SW
Silk wadding

Whaleys (Bradford) Ltd
Harris Court
Great Horton
Bradford
West Yorkshire BD7 4EQ
Water-soluble fabrics; silk organza and other fabrics

Pongées Ltd
184–186 Old Street
London EC1 9BP
Wholesalers of a wide range of silk fabrics, including silk muslin

USA

Dyes of every kind

Cerulean Blue
Dept F.A. P.O. Box 21168
Seattle
Washington 98111–3168

Frederick J. Fawcett Inc.
1304 Scott Street
Dept F.
Petaluma
California 94952

Dhama Trading Co.
Box 916
San Rafael
California 94915

Silk fabrics

Utex Trading
7109th Street (Suite 5)
Niagara Falls
New York 14301

Aurora Silk
5806 N. Vancouver Avenue
Portland
Oregon 97217

INDEX